1,001 Pearls of
Buddhist Wisdom

1,001 Pearls of Buddhist Wisdom

Desmond Biddulph

CHRONICLE BOOKS
SAN FRANCISCO

1,001 Pearls of Buddhist Wisdom
Desmond Biddulph

First published in the United States in 2007 by
Chronicle Books LLC.

Library of Congress Cataloging-in-Publication Data
available.

ISBN-10: 0-8118-5612-7
ISBN-13: 978-0-8118-5612-6

Manufactured in Thailand

Conceived, created, and designed by
Duncan Baird Publishers.

Editor: Zoë Fargher
Managing Designer: Manisha Patel
Designer: Clare Thorpe
Commissioned artwork: Sally Taylor

Typeset in AT Shannon

Distributed in Canada by Raincoast Books
9050 Shaughnessy Street
Vancouver, British Columbia V6P 6E5

10 9 8 7 6 5 4 3 2 1

Chronicle Books LLC
680 Second Street
San Francisco, California 94107

www.chroniclebooks.com

CONTENTS

INTRODUCTION

The need to look up to something greater than ourselves is imprinted in us all. When we no longer gaze up in awe and wonder, we start searching elsewhere, and this is when our difficulties begin. Within the heart of all of us is a special space, prepared for the spirit. When the spirit is undervalued, neglected and forgotten, other things come to take its place. Thus begins our wandering in samsara, constantly chasing after pleasure and security, in flight from discomfort and fear, never at home, never at peace.

The historical Buddha declared that he had "rediscovered an ancient path to an ancient city" – in other words found a way back to wholeness, to real security and fulfilment. Those who have followed the Buddha have kept the path open. The Buddha was an ordinary human being, but he was an exceptional one. His journey, as outlined in the story of his life, is strangely familiar, because it highlights all those things that are grave and true in human nature, and the dilemma in which he found himself is our dilemma too.

Did the historical Buddha really exist? We don't really know. What we do know is that the path, which certainly does exist, if followed will lead us out of suffering to happiness and the true heart's desire – the fulfilment of the human state. The word Buddha comes from the Sanskrit root *budh* meaning "to wake" – and thus means "The Awakened One". A buddha is a person who has woken fully, as if from a deep sleep, to discover that suffering, like a dream, is over. We too can wake up from the nightmare of samsara and be free.

Buddhism is not just an ancient method of transformation – it is a religion. Where it differs from other religions is in the lack of a belief in a creator God, as a permanent entity. However, Buddhists believe that wisdom, intelligence and compassion are inherent in all things, like "salt in water". They also cultivate faith, devotion and all the virtues.

As the Dhammapada says, "To do only good, to avoid doing harm, to purify the heart is the way of the Buddhas."

The word religion comes from the Latin *religio*, to "re-link". This makes us think of a path to re-link, or reconnect, with that wisdom and compassion from which we have never been separated but which we have turned away from and forgotten. The path that leads back "home" is clearly laid out in the teachings, and consists of three stages: listening or reading, reflecting upon and thinking about, and putting into action or practising. Buddhism is therefore a practical way: if it does not work, then it should be abandoned; however, if it appears to benefit us, then it can be cultivated.

At the beginning of practice, we think of ourselves as rational and reasonable. However, with a little reflection we can ask ourselves what happens when we are thwarted, when we don't get what we want. Don't we get a little heated? In Buddhism these hot-blooded reactions, known as the Three Fires of desire, anger and delusion, are seen as precious energy – not to be squandered, but to be transformed, starting with gradually familiarizing ourselves with these

reactions in the body. For this we need to be aware, and this is the reason why the cultivation of awareness is so important in Buddhism.

This cultivation is loosely translated as meditation, but in fact it starts with the cultivation of "good form", which has two aspects. The first is how we behave, and this is where the *paramitas* come in, as guidelines to skilful living. Considerable space is given to this in Chapter Two, entitled "Skills for life". With these pointers to help us, we can stop acting on impulse and practise restraint. It then becomes possible to work with our transforming energy.

The second aspect concerns the physical side of "good form": awareness of, and being at home in the body. This has a venerable history in India, from sacred dance to yoga to formal meditation practices. In fact all cultures cultivate alertness, grace and dignity of movement, but in our hurried time we forget this, and leave it to the professionals – the dancers, the gymnasts, the soldiers.

Chapter Three, "Mind and heart", looks at awareness in much greater depth. "There is no mind without a body and no body without a mind," and the healing of this apparent split is of paramount importance.

The word *karma* means action, and it is those actions that are emotionally fired that have consequences for good or ill. Sooner or later, these actions will bear fruit of one kind or another. *Karma* is utterly impersonal. It is one of the key doctrines in Buddhism and not easy to understand. This law and other important aspects of the Buddha's way are covered in Chapter Four, entitled "Finding the path". This chapter also revisits some of the earlier teachings and introduces the concept of *bodhicitta*, the aspiration toward wholeness, as well as gratitude, without which the path would be valueless. Buddha-nature is touched on, as well as nirvana.

Chapter Five, "Planet and cosmos", examines some of the ways we can look at time and our physical universe. The book concludes with Chapter Six on "The global family", which includes some of the edicts of the great Buddhist king, Asoka, who ruled a vast empire of many nations, races, religions and languages under the harmonizing influence of the Dharma, giving us an inkling of what is possible today.

The chapters cover a wide range of topics, reflecting both Buddhist practice and life itself. The Buddhist quotations selected come from all the major schools, from antiquity right up to the present. They include representative selections from the Pali Nikayas, from early Indian Buddhism, Tibetan Buddhism, the early Chinese masters and the schools of Japanese Zen. It should become apparent that despite the differences of expression, these quotations are all informed by the one Buddha-nature. Hopefully, some of these might encourage a deeper study and practice of the Buddhist path.

If this little book were to be discovered in a future age as the only record of our era, it would be found to contain the essential teachings of the Dharma as well as quotes from many sages, poets, philosophers, scientists and others, all through recorded history. It is not possible, of course, to tell from just an examination of their meanings whether they were followers of the Buddha. Some may have expressed profound wisdom memorably without leading exemplary lives. Others may have lived by the highest ideals of service and compassion. Many of those quoted – such as Socrates, Montaigne, Schopenhauer, Einstein and Yeats to name but a few – lived in widely divergent intellectual and social milieux. Yet those who choose to walk on a spiritual path or reflect on the mystery and wonder of the universe tend to find little to argue over with their companions. As the great mythologist Joseph Campbell said, "When the theoreticians

get together there is much discussion; when the practisers meet there is much nodding of heads in agreement."

My very special thanks go to my wife Darcy Flynn for her attention to detail and the selection of some of the lesser-known quotations, to Odin Biddulph, Hero Freisan, Louise Marchant for her constant enthusiasm and John Swain for his tireless help.

Dr Desmond Biddulph

Vice-President, The Buddhist Society

The Buddhist Society was established in 1924 "to publish and make known the principles of Buddhism and encourage the practice and study of those principles". The Society conducts classes in all schools of Buddhism at its headquarters in Eccleston Square, London, as well as an annual residential summer school which is held in the Cotswolds, and publishes books and a well-known journal, *The Middle Way*.

The Buddhist Society
58 Eccleston Square, London SW1V 1PH
Tel: 020 7834 5858 Fax: 020 7976 5238
Email: info@thebuddhistsociety.org
Website: www.thebuddhistsociety.org
Patron: H.H. The Dalai Lama

Life and teachings of the Buddha

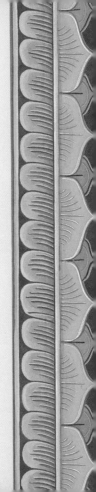

MAN, MYTH AND LEGEND

1 **Within everyone** "In this fathom-long body with its thoughts, feelings and perceptions lies the world, the origin of the world, the cessation of the world, and the way that leads to the ending of the world."

THE SAMYUTTA NIKAYA SUTTA

2 **Myth or history?** Did the Buddha really exist? In contrast to many other religions, this question is irrelevant. Legend, fact and tradition blend into a story that inspires and informs us. It has real inner meaning that bypasses the critical mind, reaching the heart, where it nourishes and helps the seeds of liberation and enlightenment to germinate.

3 **Cosmic energy** "Myth is the secret opening through which the inexhaustible energies of the cosmos pour into human cultural manifestation."

JOSEPH CAMPBELL (1904–1987), USA

4 **The real history** "I find it so tragic and ironical that the age in which we live should regard the words 'myth' and 'illusion' as synonymous in view of the fact that the myth is the real history, is the real event of the spirit. ... The myth is the tremendous activity that goes on in humanity all the time, without which no society has hope or direction, and no personal life has a meaning. We all live a myth whether we know it or not."

LAURENS VAN DER POST (1906–1996), SOUTH AFRICA

5   **A living myth** "History and anthropology teach us that a human society cannot long survive unless its members are psychologically contained within a central living myth. Such a myth provides the individual with a reason for being."

EDWARD EDINGER (1922–1998), USA

6   **A mother's dream** According to legend the Buddha's conception was miraculous. His mother Queen Maya dreamed that she was transported to a high plateau, where she lay under a

tree and a *bodhisattva* in the form of an immaculate white royal elephant walked around her three times before entering her right side.

7   **Siddhartha's family** The Buddha was born around 563BCE in Kapilavastu, a small kingdom in the Himalayan foothills in present-day Nepal, to a royal family from the clan of Sakyas. His father was King Suddhodana and his mother was Queen Maya Devi.

8   **Born in a garden** When the time for Queen Maya's confinement was drawing closer, she set out to visit her parents in the company of her sister. On the way they stopped at the Lumbini Garden and, grasping the branch of a tree, the queen gave birth painlessly from her right side to the future Buddha. The Lumbini Garden remains one of Buddhism's four holiest sites, along with the sites of the Buddha's enlightenment, first sermon and death.

9   **Seven steps** The newborn prince took seven steps to the north, south, east and west. With one hand pointing to heaven and the other to earth, he proclaimed, "In heaven and earth, I alone am the world-honoured one." This birth was the last in his long series of lives.

10   **Many names** At birth the Buddha was named Siddhartha Gautama, "the one who obtains success and prosperity". After his enlightenment, he was called Gautama Buddha or Shakyamuni Buddha (meaning "The Awakened One, Sage of the Sakyas"). The Buddha was also known as the Tathagata ("He who has come and gone"). In Buddhist sacred texts, the Buddha is also referred to as the "World-honoured One", the "Blessed One" and the "great physician".

11   A SPECIAL MAN

Neither god nor prophet, nor supernatural being, Siddartha Gautama was born, lived, taught and died as a mortal man. He was an exceptional person, who revealed a way of achieving true wisdom, compassion and freedom from suffering. According to Buddhist tradition, he was not unique – there were previous Buddhas, and there will be future Buddhas. However, it was this one who rediscovered the path to enlightenment.

12   Visions of Siddhartha's future Queen Maya died seven days after her son was born. Seers at the court predicted that Siddhartha would become either a great ruler or a Buddha ("awakened one"). The greatest seer, Asita, prophesied that the baby prince would become a great sage. Alarmed by what this news implied for his kingdom's future, the king determined to turn Siddhartha away from the spiritual path.

13   **For the benefit of many** "An extraordinary man arises in this world for the benefit of the many, for the happiness of the many, out of compassion for the world, for the good, benefit and happiness of gods and men. Who is this being? It is the Tathagata, the Exalted, the Fully Enlightened One."
THE ANGUTTARA NIKAYA

14   **In a tree's shade** One day King Suddhodana took Siddhartha to a traditional ploughing festival, a spring celebration. The child Siddhartha was placed in the cool, calm shade of a rose-apple tree while the king and his subjects took part in the festivities. Left alone, Siddhartha slipped into the first level of meditative absorption (*jhana*). Many years later, when Siddhartha began his journey to enlightenment, he recalled this spontaneous spiritual event.

15   **Worldly skills** In accordance with his father's wishes, Siddhartha was raised in the tradition of the court. He was trained in the skills of statesmanship, astronomy, oratory and mathematics, and in the martial arts of horsemanship, combat and archery.

16   **Wife and son** At the age of 16 Siddhartha was married to the beautiful Princess Yassodhara, who soon gave birth to a son, Rahula. Siddhartha continued in his life of sensual ease.

17   **Luxury** "I was delicate, very delicate. In my father's dwelling three lotus-ponds were made purposely for me. Blue lotuses bloomed in one, red in another, and white in another. My turban, tunic and cloak were all of fine cloth. A white sunshade was held over me day and night, so no cold or heat or dust or grit or dew might inconvenience me."
THE BUDDHA (THE ANGUTTARA NIKAYA)

SIDDHARTHA'S JOURNEY

18 **THE FOUR MESSENGERS**
Siddhartha spent 13 years at his father's disposal after the birth of his son. However, his serious, inquisitive nature tired of the fleeting pleasures of his princely life, and he longed for more. Although his father had protected him from the realities of life, during the prince's various journeys beyond the palace gates he saw an old man, a sick man, a corpse and a holy man. Deeply moved by these encounters, he resolved to follow the way of the holy man and find a solution to life's suffering.

---

19 **The great renunciation** On his 29th birthday, Siddhartha began the life of a wandering ascetic. To avoid alerting his father and disturbing the court, he wrapped his horse's feet in cloth and set forth with his faithful groom Channa, leaving behind his wife and son, and his luxurious former life. Together, Siddhartha and Channa crossed the great river Anoma. On the other bank Siddhartha cut his hair and beard and parted company with Channa, to whom he gave his princely clothes and his trusted horse.

20   Homeless wandering Siddhartha now lived the life of a beggar. He had no permanent shelter, and would sleep out in the open or in the shade of a tree. Dressed only in tattered robes, with bare feet and a shaven head, he travelled on foot through all weathers. He had renounced all personal possessions, and had only a bowl to beg for alms with.

21   Two teachers Siddhartha devoted himself to the teachings of two successive meditation masters. His progress was so quick and his dedication so profound that each master nominated Siddhartha as his successor. Despite having learned all that could be learned from them, including much discipline and the fundamentals of practice, Siddhartha was not satisfied, so he moved on, to seek liberation on his own.

22   **Unwavering purpose** "He presses on with his thoughts controlled, never looking back to his home, like a swan which has left its pool."
THE DHAMMAPADA

23   **Extreme austerities** After leaving his masters, Siddhartha sought liberation from suffering during six years of rigorous austerities in the company of five disciples. Meditating deep into the night left little time to eat, wash or sleep – at some points, Siddhartha ate only a grain of rice a day. Eventually his body became emaciated and turned black.

24   **Not the way** With his body wasting away and almost starved to death, Siddhartha realized that without food he would not have the strength to reach enlightenment, and so he abandoned this approach. He accepted a bowl of rice gruel from a passing herdsman's daughter, Sujata, and washed his body, hair and clothes.

25   **A man alone** Siddhartha was abandoned by his disciples, who said scornfully that he had taken to a life of ease and luxury. Deserted by his friends, his teachers and even his disciples, Siddhartha was now completely alone and without status. He decided to resolve his problems once and for all, and he settled down to meditate under a bodhi tree.

26   **Quiet abiding** "So should he sit, steadfastly meditating, solitary, his thoughts controlled, his passions laid away, quit of belongings, in a fair, still spot having his fixed abode."
THE BHAGAVAD GITA

ENLIGHTENMENT

27 **Mara's demon lookout** Long before, the supernatural Buddhist tempter, Mara, had sent a demon called Red-eye to keep watch on the bodhi tree under which, it was prophesied, a *bodhisattva* would make his bid for Buddhahood. For centuries Red-eye watched the people coming and going past the bodhi tree, but he saw nothing to disturb him. Then one day he presented himself before Mara in a state of agitation. "Why, what is it?" asked Mara. The demon Red-eye answered him: "My Lord, I have seen thousands coming and going near the bodhi tree, but saw nothing to report. But now there is a man walking toward that tree, and from the way he walks, I believe that whatever that man sets out to do, he will do. Let Your Majesty beware of what is taking place."

28 **Today, today, today** "Walk to your meditation cushion like the Buddha-to-be walking toward the bodhi tree, saying: 'Today, today, today.'"
THE MIDDLE WAY (JOURNAL OF THE BUDDHIST SOCIETY)

29	**Three temptations** Mara now sent three temptations to thwart Siddhartha in his quest. The first was duty: Mara called on him to "return to your kingdom, you have done enough". The second was sensual pleasure in the form of Mara's irresistible daughters. When this too failed, Mara sent his demon sons, who strike fear and terror into the hearts of men. They attacked Siddhartha with earthquakes and showers of rocks. Mara's temptations represent the levels of release a human being must go through before liberation – first from duty, then from sensual desire and finally from irrational self-protection and fear.

30	**The defeat of Mara** Finally Mara screamed, "Arise from that seat! It belongs to me!" Siddhartha was unmoved, and extended his hand to touch the earth, calling it to bear witness to the merit of his past lives. The earth thundered, "I bear witness to the future Buddha!" Mara was defeated.

31	**Three realizations** During the first part of night, Siddhartha understood that suffering has a cause, and expressed his understanding. Then, during the middle part of the night, he understood how to destroy suffering, and expressed his understanding. Finally, during the third part of night, he described reaching enlightenment, "even as the sun was lighting the heavens".

32   **The enlightenment** After 49 days of meditation, in the last part of the night, Siddhartha looked up and saw the morning star. He awoke as if from a dream, and he was enlightened. According to the Northern tradition, the newly-realized Buddha exclaimed: "How wonderful, how miraculous – all beings are fully endowed with the wisdom and power of the Tathagata (Buddha) – but sadly human beings, on account of their sticky attachments, are not aware of it."

33   **Clarity of vision** "Before enlightenment, all things in the outer world are deceptive and confusing. After enlightenment, we see all things as magic shadow-plays, and all objective things become helpful friends."
MILAREPA (c.1052–c.1135), TIBET

34   **Immovable** "Just as a rock of one solid mass remains unshaken by the wind, even so neither visible forms, nor sounds, nor odours, nor tastes, nor bodily impressions, neither the desired nor the undesired, can cause such a one to waver. Steadfast is his mind, gained is deliverance."
THE ANGUTTARA NIKAYA

35   **With the dawn** "At that moment of the fourth part of the night, when the dawn came up, all that moves or moves not was stilled and the great seer reached the stage which knows no alteration ... the state of omniscience."
ASVAGHOSA (80–150), INDIA

36   **The world rejoices** "When as a Buddha he knew this truth, the earth swayed as if drunken with wine, the quarters shone bright with crowds of *siddhas* and mighty drums resounded in the sky. Pleasant breezes blew softly, the heaven rained moisture from a cloudless sky and from the trees there dropped flowers and fruit as if to do him honour."
ASVAGHOSA (80–150), INDIA

37 **Everywhere** "At that moment none gave way to anger, no one was ill or experienced any discomfort, none resorted to sinful ways or indulged in intoxication of the mind; the world became tranquil, as though it had reached perfection."

ASVAGHOSA (80–150), INDIA

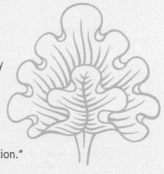

38 **Freedom** "Through many a birth in existence wandered I, seeking, but not finding, the builder of this house. Sorrowful is repeated birth. O housebuilder, you are seen. You will build no house again. All your rafters are broken. Your ridge pole is shattered. Mind attains the unconditioned. Achieved is the end of craving."

THE DHAMMAPADA

39   **Giving thanks** The Buddha
spent seven days gazing in
gratitude at the bodhi tree.
He then spent a week under
the Ajapana banyan tree,
a week under the
mucalinda tree, and
a week under the
rajayatana tree. All
nature rejoiced and
participated in the great effort
and fruit of his enlightenment.

40   **Eternal victory** "Neither gods nor demons can turn this
victory into a defeat."
THE DHAMMAPADA

41   **At peace** "My mind is hushed in a wide and endless light,
my heart a solitude of delight and peace."
SRI AUROBINDO (1872–1950), INDIA

42   **The greatest warrior** "Though one man conquers a thousand times a thousand men in battle, he who conquers himself is the greatest warrior."

THE DHAMMAPADA

43   **Dialogue with a brahmin**

A brahmin once asked the Buddha: "Are you a God?"

"No, brahmin," said the Buddha.

"Are you a saint?"

"No, brahmin," said the Buddha.

"Are you a magician?"

"No, brahmin," said the Buddha.

"What are you then?"

"I am awake."

44   **Knowing reality** "He is the greatest of men who knows the reality of nirvana, who has destroyed the causes of rebirth and broken every bond."

THE DHAMMAPADA

THE GREAT PHYSICIAN

45 **Persuaded to teach** At first the Buddha was reluctant to pass on what he had learned, thinking that people would not understand. Finally, the gods Brahma and Indra requested that the Buddha teach what he had discovered. They explained that "there are those whose eyes are just a little covered with dust" who would understand. The newly enlightened Buddha was doubtful, but at last persuaded.

46 **THE FIRST TURNING OF THE WHEEL**
The Buddha was reunited with his five ascetic disciples in the deer park at Sarnath, where he delivered his first sermon, before all the living beings of the universe. The five disciples were immediately aware that they were now in the presence of a great being, a fully-fledged Buddha. The Buddha's sermon covered the Middle Way, the Four Noble Truths and the Noble Eightfold Path (see pages 44–55). The sermon is sometimes

called the first turning of the wheel of the Dharma, and is often represented by the deer and wheel (illustrated).

---

47   **Leading the way** The Buddha continued to teach for 49 years. He addressed at their own level anyone who sought to listen, regardless of caste. Kings, princes and even murderers become his disciples, and many were led to liberation. Both men and women could be disciples, and were ordained and accepted into the monastic orders.

48 **The excellent raincloud** "As the Buddha helps them cross safely over the ocean of fictitious being, he is a steersman, an incomparable leader of those who have started their journey. He is the excellent raincloud, pouring down the cool rain of meaningful life. He is the king of physicians curing the disease of the three poisons. He is the bright lamp dispelling the darkness of loss of pure awareness. He is the wish-granting tree from which comes the happiness of all who are alive. He is the countless rays of the sun of great kindness. He is the moon with its white light of prosperity and happiness, removing afflictions."

LONGCHENPA (1308–1363), TIBET

49 **The way and the path** "Giving himself up to indulgence in sensual pleasure, the base, common, vulgar, unholy, unprofitable; and giving himself up to self-torment, the painful, unholy, unprofitable. Both these two extremes the Perfect One has avoided. He has found the Middle Way, which causes one to see and to know and which leads to peace, to discernment, to enlightenment, to nirvana. It is the Noble Eightfold Path, the way that leads to the extinction of suffering, namely right understanding, right thought, right speech, right bodily action, right livelihood, right effort, right awareness and right concentration."

FROM THE PALI CANON

50   **The fire sermon** Some months after his enlightenment, while living at Gaya, the Buddha gave the famous fire sermon: "All is burning. And what is the all that is burning? Phenomena preceded by mind are afire with wanting, anger and delusion. By seeing the cause and abhorring such suffering, the noble disciple becomes calm. The storm abated, the disciple knows no longer does chaos need to be suffered."

THE ADITTAPARIYAYA SUTTA

51   **Death of the Buddha** The blacksmith Chunda donated a dish of food to the Buddha, who was then 80 years old. Sensing danger in the meat, the Buddha asked for it to be served to him alone and for the remaining food to be buried. He ate his meal, and soon became ill. Knowing

that the time for his death was near,
he lay on his right side with his head
facing north.

52   **Last teaching** The Buddha's last
words were: "Impermanent are all
compounded things. Strive on heedfully."

53   **The final journey** According to the Digha Nikaya, on his
death the Buddha attained the four levels of meditative
absorption and entered the sphere of infinite space, followed
by the spheres of infinite consciousness, nothingness, and
neither perception nor non-perception. Finally, he attained
the end of feeling and perception, *Parinirvana* (final nirvana).

54   **Release** "Morality, absorption, wisdom and final release –
these glorious things Gautama came to know. The Dharma
he discerned he taught his monks to know. He whose vision
brought an end to woe has gone to final nirvana."
THE MIDDLE WAY (JOURNAL OF THE BUDDHIST SOCIETY)

THE CHAIN OF CAUSATION

55   **Impersonality** "Mere suffering exists, no sufferer is found; the deeds are, but no doer of the deeds is there; nirvana is, but not the man that enters it; the path is, but no traveller on the path is seen."

THE BUDDHA (THE VISUDDHIMAGGA)

56   **Causation** "The 12-linked chain of causation represents the different states of mind and heart produced by the Three Fires of desire, anger and delusion (see **58**). These passions, which are actually impersonal, can carry us away because of our attachment and the delusion of 'I'. This leads ultimately to suffering, and to rebirth. The Three Signs of Being – suffering, impermanence and Not-I (see **59**) – express this. But no state, however painful or pleasant, is permanent. It has no essence and is unsatisfactory because it changes. Through practice, we can attain true release from suffering in nirvana, the unconditioned state, where there is no longer a 'self' to cling or to suffer, or to be carried away. The Buddha taught that these universal laws are impersonal and neutral."

THE MIDDLE WAY (JOURNAL OF THE BUDDHIST SOCIETY)

57   THE 12-LINKED CHAIN
The Wheel of Life (see page 43) illustrates
the six realms of existence, the way in which
sentient beings are locked into endless cycles.
The picture shows all possible forms of life.
The six sections represent the six realms of
rebirth referred to in The Tibetan Book of
the Dead. The wheel's rim has 12 small
images, symbolizing the 12-linked chain
of causation. Grasping the wheel is Yama,
the Lord of Death. Terminating the cycle
of rebirth is the ultimate goal and Yama,
as the transformer, embodies impermanence
in that process.

58   The Three Fires Desire, anger and delusion are negative
forces, but they also represent the energy and majesty
of the Buddha-nature in its elemental state. The practice
of Buddhism is concerned with becoming aware of these

passions and calming them until they are transformed into joy, warmth, generosity, energy and wisdom. Once familiar with these forces, we can work with and transform them.

59 **The three signs of being** The Buddha said that every living thing has three shared characteristics: suffering (*dukkha*), impermanence (*anicca*), and not-I, or the absence of self or a soul (*anatta*) (see pages 60–61).

60 **States and realms** The six divisions of the Wheel of Life represent the different states of being in samsara, the world of rebirth. Clockwise from top are: the Heavenly Realms, the Fighting Demons and the Hungry Ghosts. At the bottom are the Hells. Left of this is the Realm of Animals. Finally, top left is the Human Realm. Only from here is liberation possible.

61 **The middle of the wheel** The dynamic heart of the wheel of life shows a snake, a cockerel and a pig, who are either eating each other or vomiting each other up. These animals represent hatred, greed and ignorance respectively.

THE FOUR NOBLE TRUTHS

62   **One thing only** "I teach one thing and one only: that is suffering and the end of suffering."
THE BUDDHA (THE ANURUDDHA SUTTA)

63   **The First Noble Truth** Suffering exists and all states of being are essentially unsatisfactory.

64   **Suffering everywhere** "This is the Noble Truth of suffering. Birth is suffering, decay is suffering, disease is suffering, death is suffering, to be united with the unpleasant is suffering, to be separated from the pleasant is suffering, not to get what we desire is suffering."
THE DHAMMACAKKAPPAVATTANA SUTTA

65   **Turn within** "The nature of everything is illusory and ephemeral. Those with dualistic perception regard suffering as happiness; they are like those who lick honey from a

razor's edge. How pitiful are they who cling to concrete reality; turn your attention within, my friends."
NYOSHUH KHEN RINPOCHE (1932–1999), TIBET

66   **The Second Noble Truth** All suffering and rebirth are caused by craving for existence, for non-existence or for pleasure.

67   **Never free** "We may idealize freedom, but when it comes to our habits, we are completely enslaved."
SOGYAL RINPOCHE (BORN 1946), TIBET

68   **Pointless** "A man who has had his way is seldom happy, for generally he finds that the way does not lead very far on this earth of desires which can never be fully satisfied."
JOSEPH CONRAD (1857–1924), POLAND/ENGLAND

69   **River of craving** "Like a river that when in flood submerges villages, suburbs, towns and countries, craving flows on continuously through re-existence and re-becoming. Like fuel

that keeps the fire burning, the fuel of craving keeps the fire of existence alive. ... It makes and remakes the world. Rebirth depends on the desires of life. It is the motivating force behind not only present existence but all past and future existence too."

PIYADASSI THERA (1914–1998), SRI LANKA

70 **The Third Noble Truth** The extinction of desire will bring an end to suffering and rebirth.

71 **No real power** "Enemies such as craving and hatred are without arms, legs and so on. They are neither courageous nor wise. How is it that they have enslaved me?"

SANTIDEVA (8TH CENTURY), INDIA

72 **The Fourth Noble Truth** There is a way to relinquish the constant agitation of desire: the Noble Eightfold Path.

73 **Illness and cure** "The truth of suffering is to be compared with a disease, the truth of the origin of suffering with the

cause of the disease, the truth of the extinction of suffering with the cure of the disease and the truth of the Path with the medicine."

THE VISUDDHIMAGGA

74   The surgeon's help "The Buddha is the peerless physician, the supreme surgeon. He is an unrivalled healer."

PIYADASSI THERA (1914–1998), SRI LANKA

75   Cause and effect "The happiness that we desire and the suffering that we shun come about as a result of causes and conditions. Understanding this causal mechanism of suffering and happiness is what the Four Noble Truths are all about."

HIS HOLINESS THE 14TH DALAI LAMA (BORN 1934), TIBET

THE NOBLE EIGHTFOLD PATH

76 **The way to liberation** According to the Buddha, the Noble Eightfold Path is not easy to tread. It consists of right view, right thought, right speech, right action, right livelihood, right effort, right awareness and right concentration.

---

77 **THE FABRIC OF THE PATH**
The Noble Eightfold Path can also be expressed as a continuous wheel or a single fabric, like life itself: it has folds yet is of one piece. It concerns all that we do, all that we think and all that we are. As we perceive, think, speak and act, and our perceptions, thoughts, speech and actions shape our lives, so the nature of each of our lives is dictated, and the consequences are good or bad.

---

78 **Different elements** Right view and right thought are considered to be the "wisdom" element of the Noble

Eightfold Path. The second three elements – right speech, right action and right livelihood – relate to morality or "disciplined behaviour". The last three elements – right effort, right awareness and right concentration – pertain to meditation: simply being wholly at one with what we are doing. The true expression of the Noble Eightfold Path is to see the world as it is (wisdom), to behave in keeping with the actual situation at all times (morality) and to be at one with what we are doing right now (meditation).

79   **Right view** How we perceive things conditions our actions, and the outcome of our actions can be neutral, happiness or misery. Right view is fully grasping this.

80   **Right thought** If we see the world as it is, our thoughts will reflect it. However, usually we don't – we are full of thoughts of "ought", "must" and "should", and we spend huge amounts of energy trying to square the world with our own individual view of reality. We also take things personally and feel resentful; the consequence is angry or greedy thoughts.

81 **Right speech** If we can be restrained but truthful and kind in how we speak to each other, our natural tendency to ruthlessly grab what we want from life will not take hold of us and lead to unhappy consequences.

82 **Right action** If we view the world as it is, and our thoughts and speech reflect this, then our actions will be in harmony. But because we do not feel spiritually fulfilled, we try to fill the gap with things from outside ourselves, and so our actions are not dispassionate but distorted by emotions such as anger and desire.

83 **Right livelihood** If we can avoid trying to fill the spiritual void with talk, actions and work, we shall be able to choose work that satisfies the heart, which in turn brings social harmony and a capacity not to take oneself too seriously.

84 **Being present** The meditation elements of the Noble Eightfold Path (effort, awareness and concentration) point toward a practice that eliminates over time the sense of "I",

"me" and "mine", the source of all our misery. Through Buddhist practice negative emotions are transformed into warmth, energy and the radiance of consciousness.

85   **Right effort** Cultivating right effort helps us to give ourselves energetically to each day, no matter how difficult, and to avoid shrinking from life's challenges.

86   **Right awareness** Without awareness, Buddhist practice is impossible, for how could we familiarize ourselves with the inner life and open up to our surroundings?

87   **Right contemplation** Meditation practice helps us to become quiet inside, and as we become quiet, we become aware of our bodies, feelings, perceptions and thoughts. This familiarization begins practice.

88   **The way to be** "He who is tolerant like the earth, firm as a pillar and clear as a mountain pool, such a man will never be reborn."

THE DHAMMAPADA

89   **The parable of pilgrims** Two monks on pilgrimage came to a river bank. There they saw a girl dressed in fine clothes and at a loss to know how to proceed, for the river was high and she did not want her clothes spoilt. Without further ado, one of the monks took her on his back, carried her across and put her down on dry ground. Then the monks continued on their way. After a while the other monk suddenly burst out: "Surely it is not right to touch a woman. It is against the commandments to have close contact with women. How can you go against the rules for monks?" ... and so on in a steady stream. The monk who had carried the girl walked along silently, but finally he remarked:

"I set her down by the river. But you are still carrying her."

90   **Clarity inside** "Right understanding means to understand things as they really are and not as they appear to be. It is self-examination and self-observation."

PIYADASSI THERA (1914–1998), SRI LANKA

91   **Withdrawal of mind** "I tell you that no one can experience this birth [of god realized in the soul] without a mighty effort. No one can attain this birth unless he can withdraw his mind entirely from things."

MEISTER ECKHART (1260–1328), GERMANY

92   **A need of our times** "Today more than at any other time, right understanding is needed to guide mankind through the turmoil of life."

PIYADASSI THERA (1914–1998), SRI LANKA

93   **Many vehicles** *Yana* is a Sanskrit word with a wide range of
meanings, one of which is "vehicle". The word "Mahayana",
the Sanskrit name for the Northern tradition of Buddhism,
translates as "Great Vehicle", and "Hinayana", meaning the
Theravada (Southern) tradition, translates as "Smaller Vehicle".
The term *"yana"* extends the metaphor of Buddhist spiritual
practice as a path or journey – the "vehicle" carries the
practitioner along their chosen "path". In the Lotus Sutra the
Buddha states: "There is only one vehicle (*Ekayana*) – the
Buddha-vehicle (*Buddhayana*) – the path of the Buddha."

94   **The path to safety** "This is the secure refuge, this is the
ultimate refuge; by taking to this refuge we are indeed
released from all suffering."

THE DHAMMAPADA

95   **Getting a grip** "The man who ignores the principle of unrest in things, the intrinsic nature of suffering, is upset when confronted with the vicissitudes of life because he has not trained his mind to see things as they really are."
PIYADASSI THERA (1914–1998), SRI LANKA

96   **Taking responsibility** "By ourselves evil is done; by ourselves we suffer. By ourselves evil is left undone; by ourselves we are purified. Purity and impurity are personal concerns. No one person can purify another."
THE DHAMMAPADA

97   **Weatherproof** "As rain does not break into a well-thatched house, so craving does not break into a well-trained mind."
THE DHAMMAPADA

98   **All in the mind** "The still revolutionary insight of Buddhism is that life and death are in the mind, and nowhere else. Mind is revealed as the universal basis of experience."
SOGYAL RINPOCHE (BORN 1946), TIBET

DHARMA

99   **The great law** The Buddha did not teach that a god created the universe. Rather, he pointed to a great law (Dharma) running through everything that exists. By living in accordance with this law and meeting and enduring suffering, we may achieve true wisdom and compassion, and hence ultimate freedom from suffering.

100   **TWO WORDS, TWO MEANINGS**
The name given to the Buddhist teachings is Dharma in Sanskrit and Dhamma in Pali (another ancient Indian language). Dharma or Dhamma encompasses not only the teachings but also the universal law that is inherent in all things and informs all things. With a small "d", *dharma* and *dhamma* mean the smallest elements of existence that make up a moment of consciousness such as the heat of a room, background sounds, the lingering taste of an orange you have just

eaten, the smell of incense, the thoughts you have. All these scraps of information are *dharmas* or *dhammas*. They are in a continuous pulse of movement, of coming to be and ceasing to be; nevertheless, we experience them as continuous reality.

---

101   **The Dhammapada** Translated as "Path of the Dharma" and containing answers to questions put to the Buddha in the form of 423 verses in 26 categories, the Dhammapada is often described as the Buddhist bible. The Dhammapada is a popular section of the Tripitaka, the Buddhist canon of scriptures, and is considered one of the most important texts of Theravada literature. The Pali version is best known.

102   **Proper study** "When receiving the teachings, it is important to have the correct attitude. It is not practising the Dharma properly to listen with the intention of gaining material advantage or reputation. Neither should our goal be higher rebirth in the next life, nor should we be wishing only for our own liberation from samsara.

Instead, let us listen to the teachings with the determined wish to attain the state of omniscience for the sake of all beings."

HIS HOLINESS THE 14TH DALAI LAMA (BORN 1934), TIBET

103 THE WHEEL OF DHARMA

The Eight-Spoked Wheel symbolizes the Buddha's teachings. The eight spokes symbolize the elements of the Noble Eightfold Path (see page 48–55). The swirl in the middle represents the three jewels: Buddha, Dharma and Sangha (the Buddhist spiritual community). The wheel can also be divided into three parts, each representing an aspect of practice; the hub stands for morality, the spokes for wisdom, and the rim for concentration.

104   **The first sign of being** *Dukkha* (suffering) implies attachment to those we love, to our bodies and in particular to our ideals, as well as the generally unsatisfactory and fleeting nature of life. Buddhists do not, of course, believe that life is all suffering, but instead that life cannot be all joy, as everything is transient; even in the happiest life there will be suffering, and change is inevitable.

105   **The second sign of being** We live in a universe in a continuous state of flux – this is *anicca*. Nothing remains the same for even an instant – nothing that we can hold or touch is unchanging, and yet we seek relief from this continuous, remorseless movement and even try to fight it instead of flowing smoothly with the nature of things.

106   **The third sign of being** Not-I (*anatta*) refers to the fact that we are attached to qualities and characteristics that we think of as a unity: "me". We identify with our opinions of how the world is, and how it ought to be. Human unhappiness is often caused by people defending their own or attacking

others' belief systems. But these are simply ideas and
thoughts, and we are just one human family. Fear of
the unknown and "I" are two sides of a single coin.

107 **Gone in a moment** "Thus shall you think of all this
fleeting world: a bubble in a stream, a flash of lightning
in a summer cloud, a flickering lamp, a phantom, and
a dream."
THE DIAMOND SUTRA

108 **Imagined unity** A cart (or a car) may be broken down into
its basic components – axle, wheels, shafts, sides, and so on.
In the same way different elements (*skandhas*) – body, feelings,
perception, volition and consciousness – come together to
create this deluded sense of a permanent "me".

109 **Recognizing "I"** "Whenever we get heated about something,
feel self-conscious, take ourselves too seriously, get moody
and irritable and can't throw it off, "I" is present. Practising
awareness, saying 'yes' to life and maintaining 'good form'

wear away the delusion of 'I' so that we can let go of it."

THE MIDDLE WAY (JOURNAL OF THE BUDDHIST SOCIETY)

110 Triratna The Three Jewels (*triratna*) are the principles at the heart of Buddhist life. They are: belief in the Buddha, the Dharma and the Sangha (the community of Buddhism). In the Mahayana tradition the Sangha includes lay Buddhists and ordinary people, but in the Theravada tradition it is only monks and nuns.

111 Taking refuge "I take refuge in the Buddha; I take refuge in the Dharma; I take refuge in the Sangha. I take refuge in the Buddha, the most venerable one; I take refuge in the Dharma, venerable in its purity; I take refuge in the Sangha, venerable in its harmony. I have taken refuge in the Buddha; I have taken refuge in the Dharma; I have taken refuge in the Sangha. The true Tathagata of complete and perfect enlightenment: henceforth I put my faith in him as my great Master, and shall rely on him as teacher, and not follow evil demons or other ways. Out of compassion, out of compassion, out of great compassion."

"THE THREE REFUGES", MORNING CHANT COMMON TO ALL SCHOOLS

112 **Not two** "Good friends, my teaching of the Dharma takes meditation and wisdom as its basis. Never under any circumstances say that meditation and wisdom are different. They are one unity, not two things. Meditation itself is the substance of wisdom, and wisdom itself is the function of meditation."

HUI-NENG (638–713), CHINA

113 **Everlasting teachings** "The whole world is fraught with peril. The whole world is quaking. But the Dharma which the Buddhas preach for the attainment of the ultimate goal … is immovable and unshakeable."

THE MAHAVASTU

114 **One taste** "As this great ocean has but one taste, that of salt, so has this Dhamma but one taste, that of freedom."
PIYADASSI THERA (1914–1998), SRI LANKA

115 **The blind turtle** A story in a Buddhist *sutra* illustrates the good fortune of a human birth. A lone blind turtle dwells in the depths of a vast ocean, surfacing once every hundred years. On the turbulent surface of the ocean floats a golden yoke. It is more common for the turtle to put its head through the yoke than it is for a being imprisoned in the cycle of rebirth to be born as a human who encounters the teachings of the Buddha. Human birth is like a rare jewel, difficult to find and, if found, of boundless value, because it is only as a human that one may find the path to liberation.

116 **Too much** "Sometimes when we see too much truth about ourselves suddenly mirrored by the teacher or the teachings,

it is simply too difficult to face, too terrifying to recognize, too painful to accept as the reality. And when there are things too difficult to accept about ourselves, we project them, usually on to those who help and love us the most – our teacher, the teachings, our parent or our closest friend."
SOGYAL RINPOCHE (BORN 1946), TIBET

117 **Leaving the raft** The Buddha compared his teachings to a raft carrying us across the turbulent river of samsara to the other shore, where we can find nirvana. However, once we reach the far shore, just as carrying the real raft with us would be foolish, so we must leave behind the theory of Buddhism and rely upon ourselves.

SCHOOLS AND TEACHERS

118 **The spread of Buddhism** Along with precious stones and metals, ivory, silk and other commodities, Buddhism spread along the Silk Route which traversed China and Russia and connected great empires such as Persia and Rome, and also Egypt and the Mediterranean, with the East. The faith took root in central and southeast Asia, Nepal, Mongolia, China, Japan, Thailand and Sri Lanka. The wide spread of Buddhism is traditionally likened to a lion's powerful roar.

119 **Challenges overcome** Buddhism died out in India following the destruction of Nalanda University, the great seat of Buddhist learning in India, and the widespread eradication of Buddhist practice by Muslim expansion in the 11th century. More recently, Communism virtually obliterated Buddhism in China. However, today Buddhism is thriving in Sri Lanka, Thailand, South Korea, Japan and countries in the West, and it is begining to re-emerge in China and Mongolia. The appeal of Buddhism is universal: as Albert Einstein said, "If there is any religion that would cope with modern scientific needs, it would be Buddhism."

120 **Three schools** Many schools and traditions arose after the death of the Buddha, but over the centuries most of them either vanished or were absorbed into other schools. In the first century BCE new ideas within the existing schools in India came to form the Mahayana or "Great Vehicle" teachings, which eventually became the Northern tradition of Buddhism that spread to Tibet, China and Japan. Today there are three main traditions of Buddhism: the Theravada (or Southern tradition), whose texts are based on the Nikayas in the Pali language; the Mahayana (or Northern tradition), which mostly uses texts originally written in Sanskrit; and the Vajrayana (or Tibetan tradition). Each tradition has its own history and also different schools within it.

121 **Common features** The fundamental principles of the Dharma and the *vinaya* (the disciplinary rules of monastic life) date back to the Second Council, which took place 100 years after the Buddha's death, before there was any division. The Dharma and the *vinaya* are thus common to all Buddhist traditions.

122   Mahayana The Northern tradition is so named because it was particularly successful in the north of India and in China, Korea and Japan. The Mahayana emphasizes the *bodhisattva* ideal, that each person should work for the happiness and welfare of all beings by cultivating aspiration toward enlightenment (*bodhicitta*) and the practice of the *paramitas* (virtues). Different schools (such as Zen) developed, each with its own monasteries and teaching lineages. Each school was based on one or more of the Mahayana *sutras* which stressed particular teachings, themes or ways to practise (see **133**).

123   Theravada Pronounced "terra-*vah*-dah", this school of Buddhism is known as the Southern tradition because it is most firmly established in south and southeast Asian countries such as Burma, Cambodia, Sri Lanka and Thailand. Theravada Buddhists today number well over 100 million worldwide. Theravada monks wear orange robes – perhaps the most recognized symbol of Buddhism in Western eyes.

124 **Tantra and Vajrayana** Tantra (meaning "principle" or "weave") developed in the 7th century, influenced by both Hinduism and the Mahayana. It eventually led to the founding of the Vajrayana (Tibetan) school. The Mahayana and the Vajrayana share the aim of attaining Buddhahood, but the esoteric Tantric practices claim to offer a shortcut.

125 **The Pali canon** After the Third Council, convened by Emperor Asoka of India in the 3rd century BCE, missions were sent to spread the standardized teaching of the Buddha. This teaching, brought to Sri Lanka by Mahinda and Sanghamitta, was written down in Pali in about 25BCE as the Pali canon. It is also known as the Tipitaka (Three Baskets).

126 **The sutras** The second part of the Pali Canon contains the *sutras* (*suttas* in Pali), called *agamas* or *nikayas* outside the Theravada school. When new schools developed, new *sutras* or texts were composed, similar in form to the existing ones but expounding new ideas. The word *sutra*, meaning "thread", is derived from the Vedic word *siv* – "to sew".

127 **Bon** The main religion and culture in Tibet until the arrival of Buddhism, Bon was marked by its shamanistic practices and cult of the dead. Bon was superseded by Buddhism, which became the principal religion in Tibet from the second half of the eighth century onward.

128 **Tibetan schools** The oldest school of Buddhism in Tibet, Nyingma was founded in the second half of the eighth century, during the early spread of the Dharma, by the great teacher Padmasambhava. With a particularly strong Tantric identity, and so having esoteric traditions, Nyingma does not require all its *lamas* (teachers) to be monks. The later Tibetan schools, the Sakya, Kagyu and Gelug, are collectively known as *sarma*, or "new schools". These later schools assumed political control over Tibet.

129 **Mind nature** "The nature of your mind, which cannot be pinpointed, is innate and original wakefulness. It is important to look into yourself and recognize your nature."
PADMASAMBHAVA (8TH CENTURY), TIBET

130   **Zen** The meditation school of Japanese Buddhism, Zen is
a transliteration of the Chinese word *chan*, which is itself
an abbreviation of *chan-na*, from the Sanskrit word *dhyana*,
meaning meditation, or absolute stillness of the mind.

131   **The essence of Zen** "A transmission outside the teachings,
a non-reliance on words and letters, a direct pointing to the
heart of man and becoming Buddha."
ATTRIBUTED TO BODHIDHARMA (5TH–6TH CENTURY), INDIA/CHINA

132   **The blue-eyed barbarian** The legendary
monk Bodhidharma is thought to have
been responsible for the transmission
of *chan* from India to China. His
origins are unclear – he may have
been an Indian brahmin or a
warrior, or he may even have
come from Persia. Depicted with
a beard, he is sometimes referred
to as "the blue-eyed barbarian".

133 **The mind-only sutra** Bodhidharma is said to have brought the Lankavatara *sutra* with him to China. This *sutra* is the exposition of the "Mind-only" school, which maintains that consciousness is the only reality, and that all outside objects are merely manifestations of our minds. This belief is also known as non-duality.

134 **Daruma dolls** Legend has it that Bodhidharma meditated for nine years in a cave, until he was completely imperturbable. This may explain the round, bearded Daruma dolls used to make wishes in Japanese Buddhist temples. No matter how you push them, they always come back upright.

135 **Seeds of tea** A famous legend cites Bodhidharma as responsible for the creation of tea. In his determination to avoid falling asleep during meditation, he cut off his eyelashes and eyelids. The lashes seeded the first tea bushes.

136 **Not known** Emperor Liang (or Wu Ti) was a devout Buddhist who asked Bodhidharma, "What merit have I achieved through my good works?"

"None whatsoever," was the reply.

"What then is the essence of Buddhism?"

"Vast emptiness, nothing holy."

"Who addresses me in such a fashion?" asked the infuriated emperor.

"Not known," was the reply.

137 **The sixth patriarch** Hui-neng (638–713) was the sixth patriarch of Zen Buddhism and the founder of the southern school of *chan*, which became the dominant school of Zen. Hui-neng was a poor, illiterate peasant boy from the Guangdong province of China. One day, after delivering firewood to a shop, he overheard a man reciting a line from the Diamond Sutra: "Depending upon nothing, you must find your own mind." Instantly, Hui-neng was enlightened. The verse went on to say: "All *bodhisattvas* should develop a pure mind and heart which cling to nothing."

138   **No nonsense** Lin-Chi (Rinzai in Japanese) (died 866) was a Chinese master who taught directly and simply: "When you walk, just walk. When you sit, just sit. Just be your ordinary, natural self in ordinary life, unconcerned in seeking for Buddhahood. When you're tired, lie down. The fool will laugh at you but the wise man will understand."

139   **A great reformer** Hakuin (1685–1768) lived in a remote temple and became known for his challenging teachings, which aroused the Rinzai school from complacency. Hakuin maintained, "Where there is thorough questioning there will be thorough experience of awakening."

140   **A love of Great Nature** "Zen makes a religion of tranquillity … These days human beings have forgotten what religion is. They have forgotten a peculiar love which unites their human nature to Great Nature. This love has nothing to do with human love. Standing in the midst of nature you feel this love of Great Nature."
MASTER SOKEI-AN (1882–1945), JAPAN/USA

Skills for life

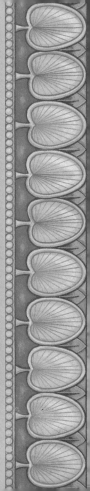

LIVING WELL

141   **Different traditions** In the Mahayana tradition there are six *paramitas*: generosity, morality, patience, energy, meditation and wisdom. In the Theravada tradition there are ten: meditation is not included, and renunciation, truthfulness, resolution, loving kindness and equanimity are added.

---

142   **THE PERFECTIONS**
The *paramitas*, or perfections, are the skills for living that lead to freedom and happiness. Cultivating them is fundamental to practice. Each *paramita* is demonstrated by the Buddha in one of his past lives, which are retold in tales known as the Jatakas.

---

143   **The importance of practice** "All those who live in the practice of the ten right ways of behaviour thereby get nearer to enlightenment."
THE MAHAVASTU

144 **Firm foundation** "As an acrobat clears the ground before he shows his tricks, so good conduct – keeping the precepts – is the basis of all good qualities."

THE QUESTIONS OF KING MILINDA

145 **Pure mind** "Just as poison spreads through the body once it has reached blood, so does a fault spread throughout the mind once it has reached a vulnerable spot."

SANTIDEVA (8TH CENTURY), INDIA

146 **Watch out!** "Just as we would quickly jump up when a snake creeps on to our lap, so should we swiftly counteract the advent of drowsiness or sloth."

SANTIDEVA (8TH CENTURY), INDIA

147 **Our effect on others** "There is a transcendent power in example. We reform others unconsciously when we walk uprightly."

ANNE SOPHIE SWETCHINE (1782–1857), RUSSIA/FRANCE

148 **Fertile ground** "When the soil of trust that is a pure mind is soaked by the rain of merit, the sprouts of the wholesome and healthy in the world grow large and the crop of excellence of the Victorious One ripens."

LONGCHENPA (1308–1363), TIBET

149 **Real skill** "What are the characteristics of worthy people? Their bodily presence inspires calmness and their actions are pure and faultless. They are wise in dispelling doubts and their words are pleasant and clear. Their mind is very calm and a veritable treasure of omniscience."

LONGCHENPA (1308–1363), TIBET

150 **Compassion** "They are learned and compassionate, their profound intelligence and their spiritual horizon is like the

sky. In their kindness they are never lazy but always diligent.
And they apply themselves to raising mankind."
LONGCHENPA (1308–1363), TIBET

151 **Strength and skill** The word "virtue" comes from the Greek
arete, meaning efficiency, being good at things. Later it also
came to mean restraint or control. In Buddhism "virtue" is to
be understood in both these senses, along with the idea of
both physical endurance and moral strength.

152 **Just-so stories** The Jataka stories are more than 500 tales,
first written down in Pali in the third century BCE. They are
a mixture of fable and folklore and are about the lives of
Buddha's previous incarnations. Each story has a moral and
demonstrates the practice of one of the *paramitas,* which
lead eventually to full Buddhahood.

GENEROSITY

153 **A smile is a gift** "Every time you smile at someone, it is
an action of love, a gift to that person, a beautiful thing."
MOTHER TERESA (1910–1997), INDIA

154 **THE FIRST PARAMITA**
Dana in Pali, the *paramita* of giving, applies
to both material and non-material things:
service of all kinds, helping others, teaching
the Dharma and, most importantly, always
giving ourselves wholeheartedly to what we
are doing right now.

155 **Priceless** "To be rich in admiration and free from envy, to
rejoice greatly in the good of others, to love with such
generosity of heart that your love is still a dear possession
in absence or unkindness – these are the gifts which money
cannot buy."
ROBERT LOUIS STEVENSON (1850–1894), SCOTLAND

156   **Heart and mind** "By selfless giving, by being generous, we cease to be niggardly and become liberal not only with our wealth but with our thoughts."

PIYADASSI THERA (1914–1998), SRI LANKA

157   **In another's shoes** "Whoever wishes quickly to become a refuge for himself and others should undertake this sacred mystery: to take the place of others, giving them his own."

SANTIDEVA (8TH CENTURY), INDIA

158 **The hare in the moon** The Buddha-to-be was once born as a hare, Sasa, who lived in a forest with an otter, a jackal and a monkey. One day, the hare resolved to offer his body to anyone seeking alms, and the god Saka decided to test him. Disguised as a brahmin, he asked the animals for alms. The other creatures offered food but the hare, true to his resolve, offered his own body. The brahmin agreed and lit a fire. The hare leapt into the flames – but the fire burnt cold. Saka revealed himself and, declaring that the hare's virtue should be known forever, marked the hare's shape on the moon.

THE SASA JATAKA

159 **Perspective**

"No one ever grew poor through giving alms."

ITALIAN PROVERB

160   **Sharing is better** "If beings knew, as I know, the results of
sharing gifts, they would not enjoy their gifts without sharing
them with others, nor would the taint of stinginess obsess
the heart and stay there. Even if it were their very last bit of
food, they would not enjoy its use without sharing it if there
were anyone to receive it."

THE BUDDHA (THE ITIVUTTAKA SUTTA)

161   **What will you give?** "In giving, a man receives
more than he gives, and the more is in proportion
to the worth of the thing given."

GEORGE MACDONALD (1824–1905), SCOTLAND

162   **Sincerity's value** "I get the illusion that
somehow, if the offering is worth more, it's more generous;
but that is not so at all."

TREVOR LEGGETT (1914–2000), ENGLAND

163   **From the heart** "The only gift is a portion of thyself."

RALPH WALDO EMERSON (1803–1882), USA

164 **Giving is joy** "All that matters is to give everything, and the quicker, the better. Fighting, struggling, rebelling and delaying make it harder but not more meritorious. So it is fruitless to multiply difficulties and delays."

THOMAS MERTON (1915–1968), USA

165 **The monkey king** The Buddha was incarnated as the king of a vast troupe of monkeys who lived near a mango tree overhanging the river Ganges. One day a fruit fell into the river and was eaten by the king of Benares downstream. It was so delicious that he and his retinue searched out the tree and camped at its base. That night the monkeys came to feed, but the king's guards attacked them. The monkey king made a bridge of bamboo between the tree and the bank of the Ganges for his troupe to escape over, using his own body as the last section of the bridge. His monkeys escaped, but the monkey king was injured, and he died. The king of Benares was so moved by the monkey king's action that he buried him with great ceremony, and was inspired by this act of generous self-sacrifice to rule righteously ever after.

THE MAHAKAPI JATAKA

166   **Benefit of giving** "It is one of the most beautiful compensations of life, that no man can sincerely try to help another without helping himself."

RALPH WALDO EMERSON (1803–1882), USA

167 **It's worth it** "The righteous man rejoices both in this world and the next; he delights and he rejoices when he sees his own good deeds."
THE DHAMMAPADA

168 **True wealth** "A man's true wealth is the good that he does in this world to his fellows."
MUHAMMAD (570–632)

169 **Donating** "The man who leaves money to charity in his will is only giving away what no longer belongs to him."
VOLTAIRE (1694–1778), FRANCE

170 **Real good** "One act of beneficence, one act of real usefulness, is worth all the abstract sentiment in the world."
ANNE RADCLIFFE (1764–1823), ENGLAND

171 **Emanations** "The scent of flowers cannot travel against the wind, but the scent of good deeds travels in all directions."
THE DHAMMAPADA

172   **Keeping your word** "Don't say that you want to give, but
go ahead and give! You'll never catch up with a mere hope."
JOHANN WOLFGANG VON GOETHE (1749–1832), GERMANY

173   **The generous prince** The Buddha's last birth before being
reborn as Siddhartha was as Prince Visvantara, who was
expelled from his kingdom for giving away an elephant
with magical powers, an act of extreme generosity. On his
way into exile, the prince gave away all his property and
wealth. Eventually he even gave away his wife and children.
However, his merit was so great that he was reunited with
them and with his kingdom. Generosity is the first and most
important of the *paramitas*. At times giving may seem foolish
and irrational, but ultimately we have to give away the whole
of ourselves if we are to be liberated.
THE VISVANTARA JATAKA

174   **Parched** "Wealth is like sea water: the more
we drink, the thirstier we become."
ARTHUR SCHOPENHAUER (1788–1860), GERMANY

MORALITY

175 **First defence** "Self-discipline, although ... not always easy while combating negative emotions, should be a defensive measure. At least we will be able to prevent the advent of negative conduct dominated by negative emotion. That is *sila* or moral ethics."

HIS HOLINESS THE 14TH DALAI LAMA (BORN 1934), TIBET

176 **Toward good** "At the root of human responsibility is the concept of perfection, the urge to achieve it, the intelligence to find a path toward it, and the will to follow that path if not to the end at least the distance needed to rise above individual limitations."

AUNG SAN SUU KYI (BORN 1945),
MYANMAR

177   **THE SECOND PARAMITA**
Sila (morality) means behaving well at all
times, living according to ethical rules or
precepts, restraint of the senses and passions,
good manners, self-discipline, courtesy,
consideration and politeness. *Sila* is also used
as a general term for the daily practice of
sustained awareness and mindful actions.

178   **A firm resolve** "I am unable to restrain external things, but
I shall restrain my own mind. What need is there to restrain
anything else?"
SANTIDEVA (8TH CENTURY), INDIA

179   **Everyday challenge** "It is easy to do what is harmful to ourselves. What is helpful and good is hard to do."
THE DHAMMAPADA

180   **Clear conscience** "He will easily be content and at peace whose conscience is pure."
THOMAS À KEMPIS (1380–1471), GERMANY

181   **Values for life** "The ideals which have lighted my way, and time after time have given me new courage to face life cheerfully, have been kindness, beauty and truth."
ALBERT EINSTEIN (1879–1955), GERMANY/USA

182   **Moral roots** "As the wind blows down a shaky tree, so temptation overthrows him who lives only for pleasure, who is immoderate, idle and weak."
THE DHAMMAPADA

183   **Admitting error** "We can be as free of regret for failure by being restored to virtue as by never having sinned. A person who sees his faults and confesses them will be pure."
ATISA (982–1054), TIBET

184   **The Five Precepts** Most lay Buddhists undertake to abide by the Five Precepts, known as the "training rules" of Buddhism. The precepts are: "I undertake to abstain from taking life; I undertake to abstain from taking what is not given; I undertake to abstain from sensuous misconduct; I undertake to abstain from false speech; and I undertake to abstain from intoxicants as tending to cloud the mind."

185   **Right restraint** "It is not only what we do, but also what we do not do, for which we are accountable."
MOLIÈRE (1622–1673), FRANCE

186   **Freedom and control** "To enjoy freedom... we have to control ourselves."
VIRGINIA WOOLF (1882–1941), ENGLAND

187   A solid basis "Moral and ethical restraint (*sila*) is the foundation of all Buddhist practice. Without it, the other Buddhist practices, including meditation, will, at best, produce only stunted growth."

BRYAN APPLEYARD (BORN 1942), ENGLAND

188   Great strength "An evil man may wish to injure the Virtuous Ones and, raising his head, spit toward heaven, but the spit, far from reaching heaven, will return and descend upon himself. Virtue cannot be destroyed, while evil inevitably destroys itself."

THE BUDDHA (THE SUTRA OF 42 SECTIONS)

189   The place to look
"Seek not good from without; seek it within yourselves, or you will never find it."

EPICTETUS (55–135),
GREECE

190   **Good habits** "Moral excellence comes about as a result of habit. We become just by doing just acts, temperate by doing temperate acts, brave by doing brave acts."

ARISTOTLE (384–322BCE), GREECE

191   **The path to happiness** "If we truly desire to be happy, there is no other way to proceed but by the way of virtue: it is the method by which happiness is achieved."

HIS HOLINESS THE 14TH DALAI LAMA (BORN 1934), TIBET

192   **Easy-going** "Moral people are unburdened with duties and frugal in their ways, peaceful and calm, and wise, not proud and demanding in their nature."

THE METTA SUTTA

193   **Morality in action** "The most important human task is the striving for morality in our actions. Our inner balance and even our very existence depend on it. Only morality in our actions can give beauty and dignity to life."

ALBERT EINSTEIN (1879–1955), GERMANY/USA

194 ADVICE TO A YOUNG HOUSEHOLDER

The Sigolavada Sutta tells of a meeting between the Buddha and Sigola, a young householder. During their conversation, the Buddha gives Sigola detailed advice on skilful living. Among the Buddha's lessons are the ways in which a man may squander his wealth, and their consequences.

---

195 The six dangers of drink

"Loss of wealth; increase of quarrels; susceptibility to disease; an evil reputation; indecent exposure; ruining your intelligence."

THE SIGOLAVADA SUTTA

196 The six perils of roaming the streets

"At unseemly hours, a man is unprotected and so are his wife, children and property; he is suspected of crimes; and false rumours are attached to his name."

THE SIGOLAVADA SUTTA

197   **The six perils of gambling** "If the man wins, he is hated;
if he loses, he mourns his loss; he loses money; his word has
no weight in a court of law; he is despised by his friends and
companions; and he is not sought in marriage, for he would
make a bad husband."

THE SIGOLAVADA SUTTA

198   **The six perils of choosing bad companions** "Any gambler,
libertine, tippler, cheat, swindler or man of violence may
become a friend and companion."

THE SIGOLAVADA SUTTA

199   **The six perils in idleness** "A man says, 'It is too cold,'
and does no work, or 'It is too hot,' and does no work.
He says 'It is too early,' or 'It is too late,' and does no
work. He says, 'I am hungry,' and does no work, or 'I am
too full,' and does no work. And while his work is not
done, he makes no money, and such wealth as he has
dwindles away."

THE SIGOLAVADA SUTTA

RENUNCIATION

200 **Perfect surrender** "Surrendering everything is nirvana, and my mind seeks nirvana."
SANTIDEVA (8TH CENTURY), INDIA

---

201 **THE THIRD PARAMITA**
The Buddha himself admitted that before he was enlightened his heart did not delight in the thought of giving up worldly pleasures. Eventually he realized it was because he had not yet experienced life without them. The practice of renunciation (*nekkhama*) reduces the pull that sensual experience has on us, leading to relief, freedom and genuine joy.

---

202 **Gain from sacrifice** "True love grows by sacrifice, and the more thoroughly the soul rejects natural satisfaction, the stronger and more detached its affection becomes."
ST THÉRÈSE OF LISIEUX (1873–1897), FRANCE

203 **Satisfaction** "Only those who know when enough is enough can ever have enough."
LAO TZU (6TH CENTURY BCE), CHINA

204 **Being content** "Have few desires and be content, because desires produce dissatisfaction."
LONGCHENPA (1308–1363), TIBET

205 **The way of the monk** "Giving up his home, the wise man will go into seclusion and cultivate delight in his detachment from the sensual world."
THE DHAMMAPADA

206 **Island and refuge** "Dwell therefore with self for island, with self for refuge, with no other refuge; with Dhamma for island, with Dhamma for refuge, with no other refuge."
THE DIGHA NIKAYA

207 **True freedom** "These days freedom is equated with doing what I want. It is hardly surprising, therefore, that our society is afflicted by so much anti-social behaviour. Real freedom is born out of restraint and discipline. This is the Buddhist way."
BRYAN APPLEYARD (BORN 1942), ENGLAND

208 **A meeting place** "Moderation is the place where all philosophies, both human and divine, meet."
BENJAMIN DISRAELI (1804–1881), ENGLAND

209 **The supreme perfection** "The person who has subdued the mind and senses and who is free from desires, attains freedom from *karma* through renunciation."
THE BHAGAVAD GITA

210 **A rhinoceros alone** "In due course, developing equanimity and compassion, cultivating sympathy with others, with love in your heart, friendly and compassionate, you will wander in solitude, like a rhinoceros."
THE MAHAVASTU

211 **A great mind** "It is the sign of a great mind to dislike greatness and prefer things in measure to things in excess."
SENECA (C.3BCE–65CE), ROME

212 **Retreat to the forest** "Delight in sensuous objects is like clouds in the autumn sky, unstable like lightning and very capricious. Give them up and resort to quiet forest groves."
LONGCHENPA (1308–1363), TIBET

213 **Strength in moderation** "A man who always lives with care, showing restraint while taking food, grows old slowly."
THE DHAMMAPADA

214 **Contentment** "Be content with simple things and free from the craving for worldly possessions."
JE GAMPOPA (1079–1153), TIBET

215 **Senses and soul** "Nothing can cure the soul but the senses, just as nothing can cure the senses but the soul."
OSCAR WILDE (1854–1900), IRELAND

WISDOM

216 **Manjushri** The *bodhisattva* of great wisdom, Manjushri, is
here illustrated riding a lion. In Tibetan his name means
"gentle friend". He provokes investigation into emptiness,
free will and the nature of self. Manjushri's fiery sword
symbolizes wisdom cutting through ignorance and illusion.

---

217 **THE FOURTH PARAMITA**
The *paramita* of wisdom (*panna* in Pali)
means seeing the true nature of things, no
longer contaminated by personal bias. With
wisdom we can then live in accordance with
things as they are, and realize inner peace
and the truth.

---

218 **Essential for enlightenment** "All the Buddhas of the past,
present and future, after approaching the *paramita* of wisdom,
have awoken to the highest knowledge."
THE HEART SUTRA

219   Spoon and tongue "Though a fool knows a wise man all his life, he will understand the truth as little as the spoon savours the soup. But when a thoughtful man knows a wise man even for a little while, he will understand as the tongue knows the taste of the soup."

THE DHAMMAPADA

220   Scents and smells "As the lotus will grow on a heap of rubbish by the wayside, spreading its sweet scent, so the disciple of the Enlightened One will shine in the darkness around him, among the refuse of the ignorant, spreading the sweet scent of his wisdom."

THE DHAMMAPADA

221   Teach without speaking "Those who know don't lecture; those who lecture don't know."

LAO TZU (6TH CENTURY BCE), CHINA

222   Our journey "We do not receive wisdom, we must discover it for ourselves, after a journey through the wilderness which

no one else can make for us, which no one can spare us, for
our wisdom is the point of view from which we come at last
to regard the world."

MARCEL PROUST (1871–1922), FRANCE

223 **Doubting** "The beginning of wisdom is found in doubting;
by doubting we come to the question, and by seeking we
may come upon the truth."

PIERRE ABELARD (1079–1142), FRANCE

224 **Every moment counts** "Better one day of wise and
thoughtful life than one hundred years of folly and
thoughtlessness."

THE DHAMMAPADA

225 **Illumination** "Just as when a
lamp is lit in a darkened room,
a thousand years of darkness
immediately vanish, in the
same way when the lamp of

the Buddha's mind illuminates sentient beings, eons of darkness are immediately dispelled."

THE AVATAMSAKA SUTRA

226 **Confidence** "The wise walk on, clinging to nothing. They are neither elated by happiness nor cast down by sorrow."

THE DHAMMAPADA

227 **Making a start** "The beginning of wisdom is this: get wisdom, and whatever else you get, get insight."

PROVERBS 4:7

228 **Self-knowledge first** "If you understand others, you are astute. If you understand yourself, you are insightful."

LAO TZU (6TH CENTURY BCE), CHINA

229 **Through heaven and hell** When the Buddha-to-be was born as King Nimi, he was so famous for his wisdom that the gods sent a chariot to fetch him to meet them. On his journey Nimi experienced all the hells and also the various

heavens. Finally he discoursed with the gods and returned
to earth. In Buddhism, wisdom means being familiar with
all states of being, and never overwhelmed by them.
THE NIMI JATAKA

230 **Up and away** "Climbing the terraced heights of wisdom,
the wise man looks down on ignorance ... watchful among
the thoughtless, awake among the sleepers, the wise man
advances like a racer, leaving behind the pack."
THE DHAMMAPADA

231 **Cheerful clarity** "The plainest sign of wisdom is a continual
cheerfulness: it is like that of things in the regions above the
moon, always clear and serene."
MICHEL DE MONTAIGNE (1533–1592), FRANCE

232 **Guard the mind** "The wise man guards his mind, which is
unruly and ever in search of pleasure. The mind well guarded
brings great happiness."
THE DHAMMAPADA

233   GENTLE POWER

Dragons are worshipped in many traditions. They represent prosperity and good fortune and are considered beautiful, friendly and wise. In Buddhism dragons are identified with Naga serpents (see page 202) and are not seen as totally mythological creatures. The Chinese dragon (*lóng*) represents the energy of heaven and is sometimes depicted grasping a pearl in one claw, representing wisdom. The Tibetan term for dragon (*Drug Dru*) refers to the sound of thunder.

---

234   Wonder opens "Wonder is the beginning of wisdom."

SOCRATES (470–399BCE), GREECE

235   Choose your teacher "The eagle never lost so much time as when he submitted to learn of the crow."

WILLIAM BLAKE (1757–1827), ENGLAND

236 **Things as they are** "He who understands the true nature of life is the happiest individual, for he is not upset by the fleeting nature of things. He tries to see things as they are, and not as they seem to be."

PIYADASSI THERA (1914–1998), SRI LANKA

237 **Eternal legacy** "If you know when you have enough, you are wealthy. If you carry your intentions to completion, you are resolute. If you live a long and creative life, you will leave an eternal legacy."

LAO TZU (6TH CENTURY BCE), CHINA

238 **Fully developed** "Wisdom gained by understanding and development of the qualities of mind and heart is wisdom *par excellence*."

PIYADASSI THERA (1914–1998), SRI LANKA

239 **Cautious and calm** "It is characteristic of wisdom not to do desperate things."

HENRY DAVID THOREAU (1817–1862), USA

240 **Courage of knowing** "Even the pluckiest among us has but seldom the courage of what he really knows."
FRIEDRICH NIETZSCHE (1844–1900), GERMANY

241 **Heart's wisdom** "Knowledge should go hand in hand with purity of heart, with moral excellence."
PIYADASSI THERA (1914–1998), SRI LANKA

242 **Inward knowing** "To understand reality is not the same as to know about outward events. It is to perceive the essential nature of things."
DIETRICH BONHOEFFER (1906–1945), GERMANY

243 **The rock's immunity** "As a rock remains unmoved by a storm, so the wise man remains unmoved by praise or blame."
THE DHAMMAPADA

ENERGY

244 **Endless renewal** "Life begets life. Energy creates energy. It is by spending oneself that one becomes rich."
SARAH BERNHARDT (1884–1923), FRANCE

245 **Pace yourself** "Far more effective than short bursts of heroic effort followed by periods of laxity is to work steadily like a stream flowing toward our goal of transformation."
HIS HOLINESS THE 14TH DALAI LAMA (BORN 1934), TIBET

246 **Act carefully** "An energetic man who is considerate in action will increase in reputation."
THE DHAMMAPADA

247 **Don't delay** "How wonderful it is that nobody need wait a single moment before starting to improve the world."
ANNE FRANK (1929–1945), GERMANY

248 **The journey, not the goal** "Satisfaction lies in the effort, not the attainment. Full effort is full victory."
MAHATMA GANDHI (1869–1948), INDIA

249 THE FIFTH PARAMITA
Energy (*viriya*) encourages us to abandon laziness and procrastination. Fear of not getting what we want can make us unwilling to wholeheartedly give ourselves to life's challenges. *Viriya* counteracts this fearful "I won't" and transforms the heart.

250 Upbeat "A person with patience should cultivate zeal, because awakening is established with zeal."
SANTIDEVA (8TH CENTURY), INDIA

251 Jump up "Better one day of energy and determination than a hundred years of idleness."
THE DHAMMAPADA

252 Premature aging "None are so old as those who have outlived enthusiasm."
HENRY DAVID THOREAU (1817–1862), USA

253 ENLIGHTENED ENERGY
The windhorse (illustrated) appears in the middle of traditional Buddhist prayer flags, surrounded by the garuda, dragon, tiger and snow lion. It embodies the uplifting energy that carries good fortune to all beings.

254 Fast track "If you spent one-tenth of the time you devoted to distractions like chasing women or making money to spiritual practice, you would be enlightened in a few years!"
RAMAKRISHNA (1836–1886), INDIA

255 A lion among deer "Abiding amidst a multitude of mental afflictions, we should be vigorous and unconquerable by the hosts of mental afflictions, like a lion by a herd of deer."
SANTIDEVA (8TH CENTURY), INDIA

256 Moving forward "Life is a progress, and not a station."
RALPH WALDO EMERSON (1803–1882), USA

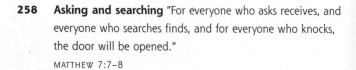

257 **Like your dream** "Deliverance depends on ourselves. There is no chance that others will deliver us, just as no one can stop the dream of a person asleep."

LONGCHENPA (1308–1363), TIBET

258 **Asking and searching** "For everyone who asks receives, and everyone who searches finds, and for everyone who knocks, the door will be opened."

MATTHEW 7:7–8

259 **Motivation** "Work while you have the light."

HENRI FREDERIC AMIEL (1821–1881), FRANCE

PATIENCE

260 **A safeguard** "Patient forbearance is the quality which enables us to prevent negative thoughts and emotions from taking hold of us. It safeguards our peace of mind in the face of adversity."

HIS HOLINESS THE 14TH DALAI LAMA (BORN 1934), TIBET

261 **Good friends** "Patience is the companion of wisdom."

ST AUGUSTINE OF HIPPO (354–430), NORTH AFRICA

---

262 **THE SIXTH PARAMITA**
Patience (*khanti*) is considered the means for overcoming anger, ill-will and hatred, maintaining inner peace and tranquillity, and tolerating the intolerable. Patience is one of the most written-about practices in all Buddhism: it calms the passions and, in doing so, diminishes our illusory sense of "I", "me" and "mine", and makes us flexible, tolerant and warm.

263   On time "Everything comes gradually and at its appointed hour."

OVID (43BCE–17CE), ROME

264   Small troubles "There is nothing that does not grow easier through habit. Putting up with little troubles will prepare me to endure much sorrow."

SANTIDEVA (8TH CENTURY), INDIA

265   Stings of speech "The fool thinks he has won a battle when he bullies with harsh speech, but only knowing how to be forbearing makes us victorious."

THE SAMYUTTA NIKAYA

266   What's the hurry? A Zen story tells of a young man who went deep into the mountains to ask a master to teach him swordsmanship. The young man asked how long his training would take. The master replied, "Ten years." The young man said, "My father is old, and I must care for him. If I work hard, how long will it take?" The master replied, "That way, 30 years." The young man was alarmed. "First you said ten years, now you say 30 years. I don't care how much hardship I have to bear, I must learn in the shortest amount of time." The master replied, "In that case, it will take 70 years."

267 **Hell is not other people!** "When we come into contact with the other person, our thoughts and actions should express our mind of compassion, even if that person says and does things that are not easy to accept. We practise in this way until we see clearly that our love is not contingent upon the other person being lovable."

THICH NHAT HANH (BORN 1926), VIETNAM/FRANCE

268 **Forbearance** "Out of compassion, the *bodhisattva* is controlled by others. Although they hold him in contempt and hurt him, he is forbearing, and takes to himself all weariness and anxiety."

ATISA (982–1054), TIBET

269 **The quiet serpent** The future Buddha was born as Bhuridatta, a serpent divinity. He was captured and forced to perform for public entertainment. Despite these and other ignominies and torments of captivity, Bhuridatta remained free of anger, and ultimately regained his freedom.

THE BHURIDATTA JATAKA

270 **Steps to insight** "I do not say that the attainment of full insight comes straight away; it comes through a gradual training, a gradual doing, a gradual course of practice."

THE MAJJHIMA NIKAYA SUTTA

271 **Little by little** "If you add a little to a little, and then do it again, soon that little shall be much."

HESIOD (C.700BCE), GREECE

272 **Welcoming the enemy** "It is the enemy who can truly teach us to practise the virtues of compassion and tolerance."
HIS HOLINESS THE 14TH DALAI LAMA (BORN 1934), TIBET

273 **Day by day** "Have patience with all things, but chiefly have patience with yourself. Do not lose courage in considering your own imperfections, but instantly set about remedying them – every day begin the task anew."
ST FRANCIS DE SALES (1567–1622), SWITZERLAND

274 **Two words** "All human wisdom is summed up in two words – wait and hope."
ALEXANDRE DUMAS, *PÈRE* (1802–1870), FRANCE

275 **Time and toil** "By time and toil, we accomplish more than strength or rage ever could."
JEAN DE LA FONTAINE (1621–1695), FRANCE

276 **The patient prince** The Buddha-to-be was born as Prince Candakumara, whose nobility and patience were so great that an official at his father's court grew to hate him. Finally, the official convinced the king to offer his son as a sacrifice. The prince faced his death calmly, but at the last moment he was saved by his mother, the queen. Her prayers were answered by the god Indra, who interrupted the ceremony.

THE CANDAKUMARA JATAKA

277 **Excellence and ease** "Only those who have the patience to do simple things perfectly will acquire the skill to do difficult things easily."

JOHANN FRIEDRICH VON SCHILLER (1759–1805), GERMANY

278 **Quenching the fire** "No more evil action exists than one done out of hatred, and no merit is more difficult to practise than patient endurance. Try to quench the great fire of anger in your effort to attain patient endurance."

LONGCHENPA (1308–1363), TIBET

279 **A quiet art** "Patience is the art of hoping."

MARQUIS DE VAUVENARGUES (1715–1757), FRANCE

TRUTHFULNESS

280   **Live in sincerity** "There is talk everywhere about worldly men's ideas and practices, which are wonderful, of course. However, you who are wise and desire liberation, do not mingle with these madmen but strive to live in sincerity."
ATISA (982–1054), TIBET

---

281   **THE SEVENTH PARAMITA**
Truthfulness (sacca) means both honesty with other people and truthfulness with oneself – being honest about what our hearts really long for and courageously pursuing this with the whole of ourselves. If we practise inconsistently, or simply because we desire praise, it will never produce real results.

---

282   **The truth remedy** "Always be ready to speak your mind, and a base man will avoid you."
WILLIAM BLAKE (1757–1827), ENGLAND

283   **Much from little** "Speak few words, but say them with
quietude and sincerity and they will be long-lasting."
LAO TZU (6TH CENTURY BCE), CHINA

284   **Ray of light** "But such is the irresistible nature of truth that
all it asks, and all it wants, is the liberty of appearing. The
sun needs no inscription to distinguish him from darkness."
THOMAS PAINE (1737–1809), ENGLAND/USA

285   **One word of sense** "Better than a thousand meaningless
words is one word of sense which brings the hearer peace."
THE DHAMMAPADA

286   **Power of truth** "A truth that's told with bad intent,
Beats all the lies you can invent."
WILLIAM BLAKE (1757–1827), ENGLAND

287 **Deceived no longer** "Deceptions cease in the realm of truth. There are no boundaries to be seen."
SOSAN (DIED 606), CHINA, THE THIRD ZEN PATRIARCH

288 **Two things** "Love truth, and pardon error."
VOLTAIRE (1694–1778), FRANCE

289 **Beyond limits** "When a great truth once gets abroad in the world, no power on earth can imprison it, or prescribe its limits, or suppress it. "
FREDERICK DOUGLASS (1818–1895), USA

290 **Longer than life** "Life is short and truth works far and long: let us speak the truth."
ARTHUR SCHOPENHAUER (1788–1860), GERMANY

291 **Indisputable** "The truth is to be lived, it is not to be merely pronounced with the mouth. There is nothing to argue about in this teaching."
HUI-NENG (638–713), CHINA

RESOLUTION

292 **One at a time** "Whatever task you first begin, bring that
thing to completion first; in such ways you will do all things
well. Otherwise, nothing will be accomplished."
ATISA (982–1054), TIBET

293 **THE EIGHTH PARAMITA**
To attain any goal we need determination.
Resolution (*adhitthana*) is sometimes called
the four determinations: for discernment, for
truth, for relinquishment and for calm. This
paramita is also concerned with perseverance,
the commitment to keep going forward in
order to reach freedom and happiness.

294 **Challenge yourself** "It is under the greatest adversity that
there exists the greatest potential for doing good, both for
oneself and others."
HIS HOLINESS THE 14TH DALAI LAMA (BORN 1934), TIBET

295 Constancy "The secret of success is constancy to purpose."
BENJAMIN DISRAELI (1804–1881), ENGLAND

296 Keep at it "Fall seven times, stand up eight."
JAPANESE PROVERB

297 The Vajra Meaning Diamond or Thunderbolt (illustrated), the Vajra is a ritual object and also the symbol of the "Diamond Vehicle" or Vajrayana Buddhist path. The Vajra represents the impenetrable, immovable, indivisible and indestructible state of enlightenment or Buddhahood ("Vajra mind").

298 Reasoning
"I am only one,
  But still I am one.
I cannot do everything,
  But still I can do something."
EDWARD EVERETT HALE (1822–1909), USA

299 **Purpose** "To greet the day with reverence for the opportunities it contains; to hold ever before me, even in the doing of little things, the ultimate purpose toward which I am working … this is how I desire to waste wisely my days."

THOMAS DEKKER (1570–1632), ENGLAND

300 **Persevere** "If we were to rub two pieces of wood together but stop and attend to something else before sparks were produced, we would never obtain fire. In the same way if we practise sporadically, for example at weekends and during retreats, but neglect our daily practice, we can seldom achieve lasting results."

TRADITIONAL BUDDHIST TEACHING

301 **Great works** "Few things are impossible to diligence and skill. Great works are performed not by strength but by perseverance."

SAMUEL JOHNSON (1709–1784), ENGLAND

302 **The right start** "Find the easiest time to begin a difficult task, because large problems grow from small ones."
LAO TZU (6TH CENTURY BCE), CHINA

303 **The rock's lesson** "Just as a rock of one solid mass remains unshaken by the wind, even so neither visible forms, nor sounds, nor scents, nor tastes, nor bodily impressions, neither the desired nor the undesired, can cause such a one to waver. Steadfast is his mind, gained is deliverance."
FROM THE PALI CANON

304 **Sisyphus, fulfilled** According to the French philosopher Albert Camus (1913–1960), Sisyphus, the ancient Greek sentenced by the gods (for trying to cheat death) to rolling a boulder up a hill only to see it roll back down in an eternal cycle, "was basically a happy man". Camus maintained that because Sisyphus had a purpose and was therefore "master of his days", he could accept his destiny with a light heart, and meditate on his situation while he walked down the hill to begin pushing the rock again.

305 Making decisions "First say to yourself what you would be; and then do what you have to do."
EPICTETUS (55–135), GREECE

306 Intoxication "It's good to apply yourself diligently to the task in hand. Intoxicated by that task, you should be completely focused, like someone striving to win a game."
SANTIDEVA (8TH CENTURY), INDIA

307 A solemn vow "From this moment until I obtain the highest enlightenment, I shall not permit ill-will or anger, avarice or envy to occupy my mind."
ATISA (982–1054), TIBET

308 Lifting the chariot When he was just a month old, the future Buddha, Prince Temiya, realized that as a ruler he would have to punish his subjects, and so he decided to remain silent and unmoving to avoid hurting other living beings. For

16 years he was tormented by trials to break his resolve. Finally, he was condemned to death. In the chariot that was taking him to his execution, Temiya finally moved: he got out of the chariot and raised it above his head with one hand, in a single action demonstrating his power and merit.

THE TEMIYA JATAKA

309 **Onward** "Some run swiftly; some creep painfully; all who keep on will reach the goal."

PIYADASSI THERA (1914–1998), SRI LANKA

310 **Self-guidance** "Irrigators guide water; fletchers straighten arrows; carpenters bend wood; wise people shape themselves."

THE DHAMMAPADA

LOVING KINDNESS

311 **Life rule** "Is there any one maxim which ought to be acted upon throughout one's whole life? Surely the maxim of loving kindness is such."

CONFUCIUS (551–479BCE), CHINA

312 **THE NINTH PARAMITA**
Loving kindness (*metta*) means "good will" in all our actions. If in all circumstances we behave with our hearts uncomplicated by our own desires, sending out good wishes and love to all beings, our actions will be kind and helpful in the deepest sense.

313 **Transforming love** "Through love we add to the fund of human happiness, we make the world brighter, nobler and purer. There is no ill luck worse than hatred and no safety from others' hostility greater than the heart of love."

PIYADASSI THERA (1914–1998), SRI LANKA

314   **Kindness is best** "You can accomplish by kindness what you cannot by force."

PUBLILIUS SYRUS (1ST CENTURY BCE), ITALY

315   **Fellow soldiers** "Always be kind, for everyone is fighting a hard battle."

PLATO (C.427–C.347BCE), GREECE

316   **Gardening** "He who sows courtesy reaps friendship, and he who plants kindness gathers love."

ST BASIL (330–379), ASIA MINOR

317   **Care for the elderly** The future Buddha was born as a young man named Sama, who cared lovingly for his forest-dwelling ascetic parents, who were aged and blind. One day, while fetching water from a pool, Sama was accidentally shot and killed by the arrow of a king who was out hunting in the forest. However, Sama's merit was so great that he came back to life, and even his parents' eyesight was restored.

THE SAMA JATAKA

318 **The way of the dove** "As the dove loves her own chicks, sitting to brood them beneath her breast, so like her, with aversion overcome, treat every creature with affection."
ATISA (982–1054), TIBET

319 **Toward the highest bliss** "Love is an active force. Every act of the loving one is done to help, to comfort, to cheer, to make the paths of others easier, smoother and more adapted to the conquest of sorrow."
PIYADASSI THERA (1914–1998), SRI LANKA

320 **Beauty revealed** "Once someone who previously did not care learns to care, they become beautified, like the moon breaking free from the clouds."
JE GAMPOPA (1079–1153), TIBET

321 **Instant merit** "Even offering three hundred cooking pots of food three times a day does not match a portion of the merit acquired in one instant of love."
NAGARJUNA (c.150–250), INDIA

322 **Quiet good** "The best portion of a good man's life – his little, nameless, unremembered acts of kindness and love."
WILLIAM WORDSWORTH (1770–1850), ENGLAND

323 **Unselfish**
"Love seeketh not itself to please,
Nor for itself hath any care;
But for another gives its ease,
And builds a Heaven in Hell's despair."
WILLIAM BLAKE (1757–1827), ENGLAND

324 **Luminosity** "Loving kindness is a freedom of the heart. It is luminous, shining, blazing forth."
THE ITIVUTTAKA SUTTA

325 **Necessities** "Compassion and love are not mere luxuries. ... They are fundamental to the continued survival of our species."
HIS HOLINESS THE 14TH DALAI LAMA (BORN 1934), TIBET

326 **Understanding** "We really have to understand the person we want to love. If our love is only a will to possess, it is not love. If we only think of ourselves, know only our own needs and ignore the needs of the other person, we cannot love."
THICH NHAT HANH (BORN 1926), VIETNAM/FRANCE

327 **Reverence for life** "How are we to build a new humanity? Only by leading men toward a true, inalienable ethic of our own. Reverence for life comprises the whole ethic of love in its deepest and highest sense. It is the source of constant renewal for the individual and for mankind."
ALBERT SCHWEITZER (1875–1965), FRANCE/GABON

328 **The heart's faith** "My religion is very simple. My religion is kindness."
HIS HOLINESS THE 14TH DALAI LAMA (BORN 1934), TIBET

329 **Everywhere** "Wherever there is a human being, there is an opportunity for a kindness."
SENECA (C.4BCE–65CE), ROME

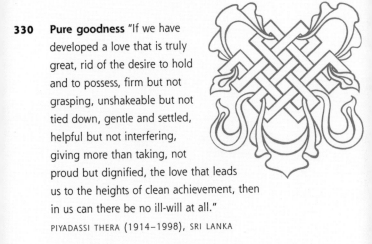

330   **Pure goodness** "If we have developed a love that is truly great, rid of the desire to hold and to possess, firm but not grasping, unshakeable but not tied down, gentle and settled, helpful but not interfering, giving more than taking, not proud but dignified, the love that leads us to the heights of clean achievement, then in us can there be no ill-will at all."
PIYADASSI THERA (1914–1998), SRI LANKA

331   **Dissolving light** "Kindness is the light that dissolves all walls between souls, families and nations."
PARAMAHANSA YOGANANDA (1893–1952), INDIA

332   **Never too soon** "You cannot do a kindness too soon, for you never know how soon it will be too late."
RALPH WALDO EMERSON (1803–1882), USA

333   **SHE WHO SAVES**
Tara (illustrated) unites the energy of all
the Buddhas. She is closely associated
with Avalokiteshvara, the *bodhisattva* of
universal compassion (see page 190), who
is dedicated to helping all sentient beings
reach enlightenment. According to one
Tibetan story, Tara was born from one of
Avalokiteshvara's tears at seeing the suffering
of sentient beings. Tara's Tibetan name
(*Sgrol-ma*) translates as "She who saves".

334   **Forever in debt** "One can pay back the loan of gold, but
one dies forever in debt to those who are kind."
MALAYAN PROVERB

335   **The eternal law** "Hatred does not cease by hatred; hatred
ceases only by love. This is the eternal law."
THE DHAMMAPADA

EQUANIMITY

336 **Oscar knows** "Nothing that actually occurs is of the smallest importance."

OSCAR WILDE (1854–1900), IRELAND

---

337 **THE TENTH PARAMITA**
Equanimity (*upekkha*) is not at all the same as indifference. It refers to imperturbability, and is one of the divine states, or *brahma viharas*. It is also considered to be one of the steps toward enlightenment. It is only when the "I" is truly vanquished that there is no fear, and all action then arises from that state of equanimity, fully aware and fully present and thus completely in keeping with the situation.

---

338 **The fourth meditation** "A monk, by getting rid of anguish, through diminishing his former pleasures and sorrows, enters

and abides in the fourth meditation, which has neither anguish nor happiness and which is entirely purified by equanimity and mindfulness. This, my friend Ananda, is the other happiness, which is more excellent and exquisite than worldly happiness."

THE BUDDHA (THE MAJJHIMA NIKAYA)

339 **Endless calm** "Profound *sutras* say that enlightenment is seeing the unseen itself, and in it there is no seeing and no seer – it is beginningless and endless calm."

ATISA (982–1054), TIBET

340 **Fearlessness** "If a man's mind is concentrated and calm, and if he has abandoned both good and evil, there is no fear for him."

THE DHAMMAPADA

341 **Equilibrium** "Develop the mind of equilibrium. You will always be getting praise and blame, but do not let either affect the poise of the mind: follow the calmness, the absence of pride."

THE NIPATA SUTTA

342 **Virtue's sanctuary** "Come what may, then, I will never harm my cheerful happiness of mind. Depression never brings me what I want; my virtue will be warped and marred by it."

SANTIDEVA (8TH CENTURY), INDIA

343 **Stoicism** "Heat and cold, the wind and rain, sickness, prison, beatings – I will not fret about such things, for doing so will aggravate my trouble."

SANTIDEVA (8TH CENTURY), INDIA

344 **Be at peace** "Let nothing disturb you. Let nothing frighten you. Everything passes away except God."

ST TERESA OF AVILA (1515–1582), SPAIN

345   PARTICIPATE
The great scholar of mythology
Joseph Campbell once said,
"Participate joyfully in the
sorrows of life" – which echoes
the Buddhist teaching that calls for
"joyful participation in the sorrows of
the world". This advice is not meant to
suggest that we try to enjoy suffering –
rather, it encourages us to recognize that
hardship and pain are an unavoidable
part of life. If we face sorrow and suffering
knowing this, we embrace the experience
of being alive.

---

346   Kingdom of the self "I am content without a kingdom and
when a man is contented in the world, is he not indifferent
to all luxuries?"
ASVAGHOSA (80–150), INDIA

347 **Stillness** "Hearing the law, the wise become like a calm, unruffled lake."

THE DHAMMAPADA

348 **Joy and woe**

"Man was made for joy and woe;
And when this we rightly know
Through the world we safely go.
Joy and woe are woven fine,
A clothing for the soul divine.
Under every grief and pine
Runs a joy with silken twine."

WILLIAM BLAKE (1757–1827), ENGLAND

349 **The essence of ease** "Walking is meditation, sitting is meditation. Whether talking or remaining silent, whether moving or standing quiet, the essence itself is ever at ease; even when greeted with swords and spears, it never loses its quiet way, and all that befalls cannot perturb its serenity."

YOKA DAISHI (DIED 713), CHINA

350   **The real cause** A hare fled terrified from the noise of fruit falling from a tree, convinced that it was the end of the world. Other animals, including deer, buffalo, elephants and tigers, asked him the reason for his fear and joined him in his flight, until a great host of animals were running for their lives. A lion, who was in fact the future Buddha, realized that the animals risked death if they continued to rush headlong toward the sea. He halted their flight with a mighty roar and questioned each animal in turn. Finally he came to the timid hare. The lion realized what must have occurred and took the terrified hare back to the tree, where he made certain that the noise had indeed been caused by a falling fruit. The other animals were reassured and calm returned.

THE DADDABHA JATAKA

351   **Unshaken, not stirred** "A tranquil mind is unshaken by loss
and gain, blame and praise, and undisturbed by adversity.
This frame of mind is brought about by viewing the sentient
world in its proper perspective. Thus evenness of mind leads
man to enlightenment and deliverance from suffering."
PIYADASSI THERA (1914–1998), SRI LANKA

352   **Pulled two ways** "The conflict of longing and loathing –
this is the disease of the heart."
SOSAN (DIED 606), CHINA, THE THIRD ZEN PATRIARCH

353   **The good sailor** "Ride your emotions as the ship rides the
waves; don't get upset among them. There are people who
enjoy getting swamped emotionally, just as, incredibly, there
are people who enjoy getting drunk."
MARY HUNTER AUSTIN (1868–1934), USA

354   **Curing all** "Equanimity is the best antidote for both
pessimism and optimism."
PIYADASSI THERA (1914–1998), SRI LANKA

Mind and heart

MEDITATION

355   **Why meditate?** "What wise man is eaten up with doubts about happiness in this life and the next? Intelligent men make meditation the essential thing."
ATISA (982–1054), TIBET

356   **No need to be a slave** "The man who has no inner life is the slave of his surroundings."
HENRI FREDERIC AMIEL (1821–1881), FRANCE

357   **Wholehearted** "Meditating earnestly, the wise realize nirvana, the highest happiness."
THE DHAMMAPADA

358   **Tick tock** "Quiet minds cannot be perplexed or frightened, but go on in fortune or misfortune at their own private pace, like a clock during a thunderstorm."
ROBERT LOUIS STEVENSON (1850–1894), SCOTLAND

359 **MEDITATION**
Translated as *dhyana* in Sanskrit or *jhana* in Pali, meditation is a *paramita* (see page 78) of the Mahayana (Northern) tradition. Meditation simply means to cultivate and develop calm and peaceful awareness, concentration and insight. Eventually, sincere and dedicated practice can lead to the ultimate goal of enlightenment.

360 **Toward fullness** "Always expand the meditating mind like the face of a waxing moon."
ATISA (982–1054), TIBET

361 **Nowhere** "One master described meditation as 'mind, suspended in space, nowhere'."
SOGYAL RINPOCHE (BORN 1946), TIBET

362 MUDRAS
Symbolic gestures made with the hands and fingers, which sometimes represent aspects of enlightenment, mudras are also often used as an aid to meditation. The seated Buddha is illustrated here with his left hand upward in his lap, and his right fingertips pointing toward the earth. This is the *bhumisparsha* (earth-witnessing) mudra, which refers to the Buddha's enlightenment under the bodhi tree (see pages 28–29).

---

363 Smooth flow "In deep meditation the flow of concentration is continuous, like the flow of oil."
PATANJALI (c.200BCE), INDIA

364 One-pointed mind "Make your mind one-pointed in meditation, and your heart will be purified."
THE BHAGAVAD GITA

365   **Direct pointing** "Over the centuries Zen has branched out into different schools, but the purpose is the same – to point directly to the human mind and heart."
YUAN-WU (1063–1135), CHINA

366   **The power of insight** "Stop talking and thinking, then there is nowhere you cannot go. Returning to the source, you gain the meaning; chasing forms, you lose the wholeness. A moment's true insight transcends all."
SOSAN (DIED 606), CHINA, THE THIRD ZEN PATRIARCH

367   **The greatest gift** "Learning to meditate is the greatest gift you can give yourself in this life."
SOGYAL RINPOCHE (BORN 1946), TIBET

368   **Don't expect results** "It is not necessary that we should have any unexpected, extraordinary experiences in meditation. This can happen, but if it does not, it is not a sign that the meditation period has been useless."
DIETRICH BONHOEFFER (1906–1945), GERMANY

369 **Heart and mind** The ancient Indian master Santideva states: "Tigers, lions, elephants, bears, snakes, all enemies, guardians of hells and demons become controlled by controlling the mind alone. By subduing the mind alone, you subdue them all." Once you have overcome your demons, they can become helpers and guardians to your meditation: their appearance is a normal part of practice, but they will eventually pass away.

370 **Bull-herding pictures** Zen uses a series of ten images known as bull-herding pictures to illustrate practice. The bull represents the restless heart, which must be found, tamed and trained by the student of Zen, represented by the herdsman. In this picture the herdsman is playing a simple tune of joy, while being carried by the contented bull.

371 **Unwavering** "To meditate, let your mind rest in its natural unrestrained and free state. By neither placing your mind on something outside nor concentrating inwardly, remain free of focus. Let your mind stay unmoved, just like the flame of a butter lamp that is not moved by the wind."
PADMASAMBHAVA (8TH CENTURY), TIBET

372 **A split-second is enough** "The merit of one who has practised meditation of profound absorption in thusness for merely the duration of a finger-snap is greater than that of one who studies for a cosmic age."
JE GAMPOPA (1079–1153), TIBET

373 **Stillness** "Just still the thoughts in your mind. It is good to do this right in the midst of disturbance."
YUAN-WU (1063–1135), CHINA

374 **For a lifetime** "A man of meditation is happy, not for an hour or a day, but quite round the circle of all his years."
ISAAC TAYLOR (1787–1865), ENGLAND

375 **The heart's lesson** "Meditation here may think down hours to moments. Here the heart may give a useful lesson to the head, and learning wiser grow without his books."
WILLIAM COWPER (1731–1800), ENGLAND

376 **Profound absorption** "Familiarity with profound absorption cuts through doubts. Other than that, nothing has that capacity. As the cultivation of profound absorption is supreme, skilful sages practise it assiduously."
JE GAMPOPA (1079–1153), TIBET

377 **Release and relax** "When I teach meditation, I often begin by saying: 'Bring your mind home. And release. And relax.'"
SOGYAL RINPOCHE (BORN 1946), TIBET

378 **The bowl of oil** "Suppose the loveliest girl of the land was dancing and singing and a crowd assembled. A man was there wishing to live, not to die, wishing for happiness, averse to suffering. If someone said to him, 'Good man, carry around this bowl of oil filled to the brim between the crowd and the girl. A man with a sword will follow you, and if you spill even a drop, he will cut off your head,' would that man stop attending to that bowl of oil and turn his attention outward to the girl? This simile shows how you should train yourselves to direct awareness of the body."

THE BUDDHA (THE SAMYUTTA NIKAYA)

379 **Signs of progress** "Health, a light body, freedom from cravings: these signs indicate progress in meditation."

THE UPANISHADS

380 **Choosing a path** "Meditation brings wisdom; lack of meditation leaves ignorance. Know what leads you forward and what holds you back: choose the path to wisdom."

THE DHAMMAPADA

381   **Good and better** "Better than knowledge is meditation."
THE BHAGAVAD GITA

382   **In the truth** "Contemplation is the loving sense of this life,
this presence and this eternity."
THOMAS MERTON (1915–1968), USA

383   **The very best thing** "Of all the excellent things there are
in this world and beyond this world, intelligent men take
meditation as the best."
ATISA (982–1054), TIBET

384   **The spirit speaks** "Meditation is the tongue of the soul
and the language of the spirit."
JEREMY TAYLOR (1613–1667), ENGLAND

385   **The contemplative**
"I go among trees and sit still.
All my stirring becomes quiet
Around me like circles on water.

My tasks lie in their places
Where I left them, asleep like cattle.
Then what I am afraid of comes.
I live for a while in its sight.
What I fear in it leaves it,
And the fear of it leaves me.
It sings, and I hear its song."

WENDELL BERRY (BORN 1934), USA

386   Absorption "The earth seems to rest in silent meditation;
and the waters and the sky and the heavens seem all to be
in meditation. On Earth, those who reach greatness achieve it
through concentration."

THE UPANISHADS

387   Training yourself "In the seen, let there be just the seen.
In the heard, just the heard; in the imagined, just the
imagined; in the noticed, just the noticed. Thus, there will
be no 'yes but': that is how to train yourself."

FROM THE PALI CANON

388   **Flash of immortality** "The practice of self-realization leads to a discovery of something immortal, the undying in the dying. All thoughts and feelings rise and pass away."
TREVOR LEGGETT (1914–2000), ENGLAND

389   **Free the mind** "When the mind is free from desires, concentration arises naturally, no matter what activity you are engaged in."
AJAHN CHAH (1918–1981), THAILAND

390   **No action** "What should we 'do' with the mind in meditation? Nothing. Just leave it, simply, as it is."
SOGYAL RINPOCHE (BORN 1946), TIBET

391   **Oneness** "The meditator cultivates at-oneness, which ends in the destruction of greed, anger and delusion ... at-oneness has the deathless as its aim ... at-oneness flows into nirvana, slides to nirvana, tends to nirvana."
THE SAMYUTTA NIKAYA

392 **Tame the mind** "If the inner mind has been tamed, the outer enemy cannot harm you."
ATISA (982–1054), TIBET

393 **Protection** "A meditation technique used in Tibetan Buddhism is uniting the mind with the sound of a mantra. The definition of mantra is 'that which protects the mind'."
SOGYAL RINPOCHE (BORN 1946), TIBET

394 **Single-mindedness** A Zen monk retreated to a solitary mountain to meditate, but found it difficult to concentrate. One evening he saw a tiger crouched in nearby bushes. If he moved, the tiger would attack him – he had to remain still, in total absorption. When dawn came, the tiger gave up and left. The next two nights, the monk sat in the same place, and the tiger returned. At dawn on the third day, the monk experienced a great awakening, collapsed and died. At his funeral, a tiger was seen watching in the distance.

AWARENESS

395   **The four postures** "When walking, a *bhikkhu* [fully ordained monk] knows: 'I am walking;' when standing, he knows: 'I am standing;' when sitting, he knows: 'I am sitting;' when lying down, he knows: 'I am lying down'. In this way he knows the body as a body, both internally and externally, independent, not clinging to anything in the world."
THE SATIPATTHANA SUTTA

396   **Watchful, heedful** "Watchfulness is the path to immortality, and heedlessness the path to death. The watchful do not die, but the heedless are already like the dead."
THE DHAMMAPADA

397   **The spirit's silence** "I have thrown from me the whirling dance of mind and stand now in the spirit's silence, free."
SRI AUROBINDO (1872–1950), INDIA

398   **End of playtime** "Thou shalt not let thy senses make a playground of thy heart and mind."
TIBETAN BUDDHIST TEACHING

399 **Lightning** "What a lightning flash in the gloom it is for the self, cloaked in the darkness of ignorance, when awareness is gained even a little bit!"
ATISA (982–1054), TIBET

400 **Vividly awake, free and easy** "Don't accept the pleasant or reject the awful, don't affirm or deny, but remain vividly awake in the state of unfabricated naturalness! By remaining like this, the sign of progress is that your body, speech and mind feel free and easy, beyond pleasure and pain."
PADMASAMBHAVA (8TH CENTURY), TIBET

401 **Expecting the dawn** "We must learn to reawaken and keep ourselves awake, not by mechanical aid but by an infinite expectation of the dawn."
HENRY DAVID THOREAU (1817–1862), USA

402 LORD OF THE BIRDS
The garuda is a mythical bird, the celestial hawk of Indian mythology. Its upper torso and arms are of a man, and it has the head, beak and legs of a bird, with wings coming from the middle of its back. It hatches fully grown from an egg and is immediately able to fly. The garuda symbolizes the fully aware, awakened state of Buddha-mind. It destroys five snakes, which represent the physical and psychological diseases to which all sentient beings are prey.

---

403 Wholehearted looking "Without asking about past or future, here and now, just look! What is this? What truly is this 'I' who asks? Who sees, hears, feels and knows? Who walks, stands, sits and lies down? Or moves about restlessly? At all times, in all places, look with all your heart and do not give up looking for one moment. For this kind of looking,

neither reasons nor explanations are needed. Just wholeheartedly look. Thus you smash the ball of doubt."
MASTER DAIBI (1882–1964), JAPAN

404   **The lama in the heart** "As pure awareness is the real Buddha, in openness and contentment I found the *lama* in my heart. When we realize that this unending natural mind is the very nature of the *lama*, then there is no need for attached, grasping or weeping prayers or complaints."
DUDJOM RINPOCHE (1904–1987), TIBET

405   **Leading the elephant** "If the elephant of the mind is completely restrained by the rope of mindfulness, then all perils vanish and complete well-being is obtained."
SANTIDEVA (8TH CENTURY), INDIA

406   **The runaway mind** "The undisciplined mind is the source of all our troubles which do not fall into the category of unavoidable suffering such as sickness, old age and death."
HIS HOLINESS THE 14TH DALAI LAMA (BORN 1934), TIBET

407   **Only one thing** "A hundred things may be explained to you, a thousand things told, but one thing only should you grasp. Know one thing and everything is freed – remain within your inner nature, your awareness."

PADMASAMBHAVA (8TH CENTURY), TIBET

408   **Seat of enlightenment** "Do not build up your views upon your senses and thoughts; but at the same time do not seek the mind away from your senses and thoughts, do not try to grasp reality by rejecting your senses and thoughts. When you are neither attached to nor detached from them, then you enjoy perfect unobstructed freedom, then you have the seat of enlightenment."

HUANG-PO HSI-YUAN (9TH CENTURY), CHINA

409   **Overcoming** "There is no allurement or enticement, actual or imaginary, which a well-disciplined mind may not surmount. The wish to resist more than half-accomplishes the object."

CHARLOTTE DACRE (1782–1841), ENGLAND

410 Good days and bad days "For a long time, meditation, like all forms of training, will have good days and bad days: sometimes it will be only 20% successful, but sometimes 80%. A lot depends on how the daily life is lived. If selfishness is reduced to some extent externally, it will not return to disturb the meditation."
TREVOR LEGGETT (1914–2000), ENGLAND

411 Always present "Integral awareness is fluid and adaptable, present in all places and at all times."
LAO TZU (6TH CENTURY BCE), CHINA

412 Just ourselves "The spiritual man is not dependent upon externals. When there is nothing to screen oneself from outside views, one comes to oneself. This is where we stand free from distinctions and discriminations."
D.T. SUZUKI (1870–1966), JAPAN

413 **Inspired awareness** "When you are inspired by some great purpose, all your thoughts break their bonds. Your mind transcends limitations, your consciousness expands in every direction and you find yourself in a new, great and wonderful world. Dormant forces, faculties and talents become alive, and you discover yourself to be a greater person by far than you ever dreamed yourself to be."
PATANJALI (C.200BCE), INDIA

414 **To infinity** "Meditation is the dissolution of thoughts in pure consciousness without objectification, knowing without thinking, merging finitude in infinity."
SWAMI SIVANANDA (1887–1963), INDIA

415 **Supreme treasure** "The wise man regards watchfulness as his greatest treasure."
THE DHAMMAPADA

416   **All-knowing** Longchenpa was a 14th-century Tibetan
Buddhist master and scholar. He trained under the leading
teachers of his age and produced more than 250 works
exploring Buddhism. Longchenpa achieved the title
kun-mkhyen, or "all-knowing". He spent most of his life as
a wandering political exile or in retreat. Pearls **417–423**
explore his ideas of the nature of the meditating mind.

417   **Ocean** "Let it be, lustrous smooth like the ocean, without
waves, free from the slime of subject and object."
LONGCHENPA (1308–1363), TIBET

418   **Mountain** "Let it be, firm and unshaking like a mountain,
without expectations and fears, without affirmation and
negation."
LONGCHENPA (1308–1363), TIBET

419   **Sky** "Let it be, open and bright like the sky, without taking
sides, with no clouds of concepts."
LONGCHENPA (1308–1363), TIBET

420 **Mirror** "Let it be, clear and bright like a mirror."
LONGCHENPA (1308–1363), TIBET

421 **Rainbow** "Let it be, like the rainbow, complete and free-standing from the moment it appears, clear and bright with neither elation nor depression upsetting it."
LONGCHENPA (1308–1363), TIBET

422 **Archer** "Let it be, like an archer undistracted, in that natural pristine awareness, neither stretching nor slackening, poised at full stretch."
LONGCHENPA (1308–1363), TIBET

423 **Completion** "Let it be, like someone who has finished his work and knows so for certain, spontaneously present, without expectations or fears."
LONGCHENPA (1308–1363), TIBET

INNER PEACE

424   **The supreme goal** "But I deem the highest goal of a man to be the stage in which there is neither old age, nor fear, nor disease, nor birth, nor death, nor anxieties, and in which there is not continuous renewal of activity."
ASVAGHOSA (80–150), INDIA

425   **Earthly peace** "What life can compare with this? Sitting quietly by the window, I watch leaves fall and the flowers bloom as the seasons come and go."
SECCHO (982–1052), CHINA

426   **Passions at heaven's gates** "Those who enter the gates of heaven are not beings who have no passions or who have curbed the passions, but those who have cultivated an understanding of them."
WILLIAM BLAKE (1757–1827), ENGLAND

427   **Quiet focus** "True tranquillity is found in activity, in the midst of sense-objects."
AJAHN CHAH (1918–1981), THAILAND

428 **Stop and realize** "Stopping is an entrance into the wonderful silence and peacefulness of potentiality; and realizing is an entrance into the riches of intuition and transcendental intelligence."
MASTER CHIH-I (538–597), JAPAN

429 **The way of compassion** "I attribute my sense of peace to the effort to develop concern for others."
HIS HOLINESS THE 14TH DALAI LAMA (BORN 1934), TIBET

430 **Opportunities** "There is none more stupid than he who, having become a human being, does not practise what is wholesome; he merely wastes his unique occasion and right juncture. Therefore, always engage in the quest for life's meaning, which is inner peace."
LONGCHENPA (1308–1363), TIBET

431 **A winged moment** "Didst thou ever descry a glorious eternity in a winged moment of time? Didst thou ever see a bright infinite in the narrow point of an object? Then thou

knowest what spirit means – the spire top whither all
things ascend harmoniously and where they meet and
sit contented in an unfathomed depth of life."
PETER STERRY (1613–1672), ENGLAND

432 **Total harmony** "He who lives in harmony with himself lives
in harmony with the world."
MARCUS AURELIUS (121–180), ROME

433 **Pure vastness** "The mind should be a vastness like the sky.
Mental events should be allowed to disperse like clouds."
LONGCHENPA (1308–1363), TIBET

434 **The heart of happiness** "The principal characteristic of
genuine happiness is peace: inner peace."
HIS HOLINESS THE 14TH DALAI LAMA (BORN 1934), TIBET

435 **Serenity** "You cannot perceive beauty
but with a serene mind."
HENRY DAVID THOREAU (1817–1862), USA

EMPTINESS

436 **Everything is Zen** "Not thinking about anything is Zen. Once you know this, walking, standing, sitting or lying down, everything you do is Zen. To know that the mind is empty is to see the Buddha. ... Using the mind to look for reality is delusion. Not using the mind to look for reality is awareness. Freeing yourself from words is liberation."
BODHIDHARMA (5TH–6TH CENTURY), INDIA/CHINA

---

437 **THE PARABLE OF THE CLOTH**
The parable of a piece of cloth shows that we must empty the mind and heart in order to practise. The Buddha said: "Suppose a piece of cloth were stained when the dyer dipped it into the dye. It would look poorly dyed because of the

MIND AND HEART – emptiness 178/179

cloth's impure colour. However, if the piece of cloth were pure and bright when the dyer dipped it into the dye, it would look well-dyed because of the cloth's pure colour. What are the imperfections that defile the heart and mind? Desire, ill-will, anger, revenge, vanity, contempt, arrogance, envy, avarice, deceit, conceit, negligence, sloth, doubt and agitation."

---

438   **Quiet mind** "Like a thief entering an empty house, bad thoughts cannot in any way harm an empty mind."
PADMASAMBHAVA (8TH CENTURY), TIBET

439   **Encourage the mind** "When a depressing thought occurs, encourage the mind with loftiness. Continually cultivate emptiness. Whenever objects of love or hate arise, look upon them as illusory creations."
ATISA (982–1054), TIBET

440   **Still your mind** "Do not think about the thinkable. Do not think about the unthinkable. By thinking about neither the thinkable nor the unthinkable, you will see voidness."
JE GAMPOPA (1079–1153), TIBET

441   **Song of enlightenment** "You cannot grasp it; nor can you get rid of it. In not being able to reach it, you reach it. When you speak, it is silent; when you are silent, it speaks."
YUNG CHIA (665–713), CHINA

442   **A breath of Zen** "Fidelity to grace in my life is fidelity to simplicity, rejecting ambition and analysis and elaborate thought, or even elaborate concern. A breath of Zen blows all these cobwebs out the window."
THOMAS MERTON (1915–1968), USA

443   **The void** "All beings arise from space, and into space they return; space is indeed their beginning, and space is their final end."
THE UPANISHADS

444   **No concepts** "All things have the character of emptiness,
they have no beginning, no end, they are faultless and not
faultless, they are not imperfect and not perfect. Therefore,
in this emptiness there is no form, no perception, no name,
no concepts, no knowledge."
THE HEART SUTRA

445   **Fear of freedom** "What makes us afraid is our great
freedom in the face of the emptiness that has still to
be filled."
KARL JASPERS (1883–1969),
GERMANY

446   **Root and origin**
"Allow the heart to
empty itself of all
turmoil! Retrieve
the tranquillity of
mind from which
you issued. Although

all forms are dynamic and we all
grow and transform, each of us is
compelled to return to our root.
Our root is quietude. To fully return
to our root is to be enlightened."
LAO TZU (6TH CENTURY BCE), CHINA

447 **Mundane things** "There are no mundane things outside
of Buddhism, and there is no Buddhism outside of
mundane things."
YUAN-WU (1063–1135), CHINA

448 **The spirit's ear** "Inner unity ... means hearing, but not with
the ear; hearing, but not with the understanding; hearing
with the spirit, with your whole being. ... The hearing of the
spirit is not limited to any one faculty, to the ear, or to the
mind. Hence it demands the emptiness of all the faculties.
And when the faculties are empty, then the whole being
listens. There is a direct grasp of what is there before you."
CHUANG TZU (369–286), CHINA

449   **Opening and letting go** "Zen requires opening the heart
and mind and losing all false cognition and false views.
When nothing hangs on your mind and you have passed
through clearly, then you are ready for refinement."
YUAN-WU (1063–1135), CHINA

450   **Into thin air**
"These are our actors,
As I foretold you were all spirits and
Are melted into air, into thin air:
... And, like this insubstantial pageant faded,
Leave not a rack behind:
We are such stuff
As dreams are made on, and our little life
Is rounded with a sleep."
WILLIAM SHAKESPEARE (1564–1616), ENGLAND; FROM *THE TEMPEST*

451   **Effortless action** "Act without acting on. Work without
working at."
LAO TZU (6TH CENTURY BCE), CHINA

CHOICELESSNESS

452 **Picking and choosing** "The Great Way is not difficult: it only avoids picking and choosing."

SOSAN (DIED 606), CHINA, THE THIRD ZEN PATRIARCH

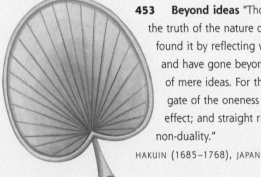

453 **Beyond ideas** "Those who testify to the truth of the nature of the Self have found it by reflecting within themselves, and have gone beyond the realm of mere ideas. For them opens the gate of the oneness of cause and effect; and straight runs the path of non-duality."

HAKUIN (1685–1768), JAPAN

454 **Avoiding karma** "*Karma* is about choice. We can go up or down, to the heavens or the hells. We are arbiters of our own fate. With the Buddha's help we can avoid these realms by not creating any *karma*. This is salvation. This is the Middle Path."

BRYAN APPLEYARD (BORN 1942), ENGLAND

455 NO CHOICE, EVERY CHOICE

In Buddhism, choicelessness means acting in harmony with clear-minded awareness. Rather than "blowing with the wind" or being the victims of whim, we act spontaneously, which enables us to "get on with things" naturally and live well.

456 Reincarnated choice "One teacher used to say: 'We have all been Nero, we have all been Judas, we have all been Hulagu, who burnt Baghdad and many of its citizens alive. Now we have a choice again. What will we decide to be now?' The Buddha stands before us saying: 'Will you not walk with me this time?'"

TREVOR LEGGETT (1914–2000), ENGLAND

COMPASSION

457 **Feel deeply** "The more we know, the better we forgive.
Those who feel deeply feel for all living beings."
MADAME DE STAËL (1766–1817), FRANCE

458 **COMPASSION FOR OURSELVES**
The Dalai Lama has said that if compassion
does not extend to ourselves, it is not complete.
If we see ourselves as equal to everyone
else, it is easier to love others. And
when we understand that others'
longing for happiness is as great
as our own, it is easier to wish all
sentient beings well.

459 **Your own value** "Lack of proper recognition of your own
value is always harmful and can lead to a state of mental,
emotional and spiritual paralysis."
HIS HOLINESS THE 14TH DALAI LAMA (BORN 1934), TIBET

460   Song of experience

"Can I see another's woe,
And not be in sorrow too?
Can I see another's grief
And not seek for kind relief?"

WILLIAM BLAKE (1757–1827), ENGLAND

461   Compassion in our bones "Great compassion penetrates
into the marrow of the bone. It is the support of all living
beings. Like the love of a father for his only son, the
tenderness of a Buddha is all-pervasive."

NAGARJUNA (c.150–250), INDIA

462   Gardening from the refuge

"A man who, by having taken
refuge, has become the site
of spiritual growth will
cultivate his mind for the
welfare of those who are
alive, by letting the flower

of compassion blossom in the soil of love and tending it with the pure water of equanimity in the cool shade of joyfulness."

LONGCHENPA (1308–1363), TIBET

463 **Priorities** "Three things in human life are important. The first is to be kind. The second is to be kind. And the third is to be kind."

HENRY JAMES (1843–1916), USA/ENGLAND

464 **Freedom from self** "Compassion has been achieved when we have cast off the shackles of cherishing ourself more than others and there is a real, rather than verbal, longing that all beings may be liberated from suffering."

JE GAMPOPA (1079–1153), TIBET

465 **A CONSEQUENCE OF REBIRTH**
Buddhism teaches that unless someone
reaches enlightenment in this lifetime, they
will be reborn. If we are all reincarnated, it
is possible that those whom we do not like
or even know may have been our parents,
family or friends in a former life. Meditating
on this makes it easier to feel compassion.

---

466 **Exclude none** "Were our own mother to be tormented by
hunger and thirst, full of fear, completely disheartened,
would we not feel very much compassion for her? Those
deprived spirits who suffer torments like these have all been
our own mothers. How can we not feel compassion?"
JE GAMPOPA (1079–1153), TIBET

467 **A problem shared** "By compassion we make others' misery
our own, and so, by relieving them, we relieve ourselves."
THOMAS BROWNE (1605–1682), ENGLAND

468 **A COMPASSIONATE BEING**
Avalokiteshvara (illustrated) is the Buddhist embodiment of compassion, who guards the world in the interval between the Buddha Shakyamuni and the future Buddha Maritreya. He made a vow that he would not rest until he had liberated every being from all the realms of suffering. He is known by many different names, and is often shown with many arms and many heads so that he can work with myriad beings at the same time.

---

469 **God's wisdom** "Man may dismiss compassion from his heart, but God never will."

WILLIAM COWPER (1731–1800), ENGLAND

470 **Sun, moon and sky** "Compassion is the wish-fulfilling gem, the auspicious jar from which the splendour of good fortune comes;

it is the finest medicine from which happiness derives, because the disease of living beings is cured. It is the sun of pristine cognitions, the moon soothing afflictions. It is like the sky, studded with the stars of spotless qualities, always bringing about prosperity and bliss."

LONGCHENPA (1308–1363), TIBET

471 **From compassion to enlightenment** "Out of the thought of love comes the thought of compassion, and from the thought of compassion the thought of enlightenment emerges."

ATISA (982–1054), TIBET

472 **Solid start** "Compassion is the basis of morality."

ARTHUR SCHÖPENHAUER (1788–1860), GERMANY

473 **Better than understanding** "I would rather feel compassion than know the meaning of it."
ST THOMAS AQUINAS (1225–1274), ITALY

474 **The heart to help** "He has the right to criticize who has the heart to help."
ABRAHAM LINCOLN (1809–1865), USA

475 **A distinction** "It is important not to allow ourselves to be put off by the magnitude of others' suffering. The misery of millions is not a cause for pity. Rather it is a cause for compassion."
HIS HOLINESS THE 14TH DALAI LAMA (BORN 1934), TIBET

476 **The best medicine** "Compassion will cure more sins than condemnation."
HENRY WARD BEECHER (1813–1887), USA

477 **Dewdrop** "The dew of compassion is a tear."
LORD BYRON (1788–1824), ENGLAND

FORTITUDE

478   **Tough target** "As the elephant endures an arrow, so will I patiently bear abuse, for many in the world are unkind."
THE DHAMMAPADA

479   **A river rising** "Fortitude implies a firmness and strength of mind that enables us to do and suffer as we ought. It rises upon an opposition and, like a river, swells the higher for having its course stopped."
JEREMY COLLIER (1650–1726), ENGLAND

480   **Swordplay** "We should ward off the blows of mental afflictions and severely attack them, as if engaged in a sword-fight with a trained enemy."
SANTIDEVA (8TH CENTURY), INDIA

481   **Let's get real** "Old age is no place for sissies."
BETTE DAVIS (1908–1989), USA

482   **Brave heart** "Courage is knowing what not to fear."
PLATO (C.427–347BCE), GREECE

483   **Don't be deceived** "Fear is only as deep as the mind allows."

JAPANESE PROVERB

484   **The way of the camel** "As a camel bears its work, and heat, and hunger, and thirst, through deserts of sand and faints not, so the fortitude of a man sustains him through all perils."

JOHN RUSKIN (1819–1900), ENGLAND

485   **Steering a course** "Whatever you do, you need courage. Whatever course you decide upon, there is always someone to tell you that you are wrong."

RALPH WALDO EMERSON (1803–1882), USA

486   **Standing firm** "As the wind that does not throw down the mountains, temptation does not overthrow him who lives without looking for pleasure, who is moderate, faithful and strong."

THE DHAMMAPADA

487 **Solid** "Bravery is stability, not of legs and arms, but of courage and the soul."
MICHEL DE MONTAIGNE (1533–1592), FRANCE

488 **True gold** "Testing purifies the gold by boiling the scum away."
JALAL UD-DIN RUMI (1207–1273), PERSIA

489 **Lessons of suffering** "The cause of happiness comes rarely, and many are the seeds of suffering! Yet if I have no pain, I'll never long for freedom. Therefore, O my mind, be firm!"
SANTIDEVA (8TH CENTURY), INDIA

490 **Classical maxim** "*Fortis fortuna adiuvat.* Fortune assists the brave."
TERENCE (c.190–159BCE), ROME

491 **Embrace life, embrace death** "The child in the womb does not know what will come after birth. He must be born in order to live. I am here to learn to face death as my birth."
THOMAS MERTON (1915–1968), USA

492 **Acceptance** "Be willing to have it so. Acceptance of what has happened is the first step to overcoming the consequences of any misfortune."
WILLIAM JAMES (1842–1910), USA

493 **Self-possession** "True fortitude I take to be the quiet possession of a man's self and an undisturbed doing of his duty, whatever evils beset or dangers lie in his way."
JOHN LOCKE (1632–1704),
ENGLAND

494   **Making the best of things** "The ideal man bears the accidents of life with dignity and grace, making the best of circumstances."
JOSEPH ADDISON (1672–1719), ENGLAND

495   **The greatest virtue** "Courage is reckoned the greatest of all virtues because unless a man has that virtue, he has no security for preserving any other."
SAMUEL JOHNSON (1709–1784), ENGLAND

496   **Meant to be** "Nothing happens to anybody which he is not fitted by nature to bear."
MARCUS AURELIUS (121–180), ROME

497   **Testing point** "Courage is not simply one of the virtues, but the form of every virtue at the testing point, which means, at the point of highest reality."
C.S. LEWIS (1898–1963), ENGLAND

498   IS THAT SO?

The Zen Master Hakuin was honored by his neighbours as one who led a pure life. One day a beautiful girl who lived near him was found to be pregnant. Her parents were very angry. At first the girl would not say who the father was, but in answer to pressure, she finally named Hakuin. Her parents furiously accused Hakuin, but all he would say was, "Is that so?" When the baby was born it was taken to Hakuin, who took great care of the child. From his neighbours he obtained milk and everything else the child needed. A year later the girl could stand it no longer, so she told her parents the truth – the real father was a young man who worked in the fish market. The girl's parents immediately confessed and apologized to Hakuin – but all he said was, "Is that so? Now take your baby home and take very good care of him."

WHOLEHEARTEDNESS

499 **Don't wobble** "When sitting, sit; when standing, stand. Above all, don't wobble."
ZEN SAYING

500 **Deep action** "When you do something, you should burn yourself completely, like a good bonfire, leaving no trace of yourself."
SHUNRYU SUZUKI (1904–1971), JAPAN

501 **Faith and heart** "It is faith in something and enthusiasm for something that make a life worth living."
OLIVER WENDELL HOLMES (1809–1894), USA

502 **Pure rejoicing** "Whether rejoicing in everyone's virtue or rejoicing in our own virtue, when the yogi sees these as the same, that is pure rejoicing."
ATISA (982–1054), TIBET

503 **Total way** "Wheresoever you go, go with all your heart."
CONFUCIUS (551–479BCE), CHINA

504 **Feel the heat** "With Buddhist theory we are like armchair travellers viewing some exotic, tropical landscape: we sit in a cool room, untouched by the scorching sun. But in practice the pretty pictures must go and we really feel the heat."
BRYAN APPLEYARD (BORN 1942), ENGLAND

505 **All one** "Thou shalt not separate thy being from the rest, but merge the ocean within the drop, the drop with the ocean."
TIBETAN BUDDHIST TEACHING

506 **Bath time** "A man who, although he has learned to abstain from overt immoral acts, still persists in nursing ill-will, harms himself by throwing dirt over himself, like an elephant after his bath."
ASVAGHOSA (80–150), INDIA

507 **Be aware** "Each activity done in full awareness, for its own sake, is an expression of our practice, of our Dharma."
AJAHN CHAH (1918–1981), THAILAND

508   **The naga-monk** In Buddhism half-human, half-snake *nagas* can transform into humans. A legend tells of a *naga* in human form who was ordained as a monk. He was discovered by the Buddha, who forbade him to remain a monk. The *naga* was so sad not to be able to pursue enlightenment that out of compassion the Buddha taught him the Five Precepts, so that he could attain a human existence in his next life.

509   **Complete effort** "Whatever you do, do it with all your might."
CICERO (c.106–43BCE), ROME

510 **Enthusiasm** "The sense of this word in Greek affords us the noblest definition of it; enthusiasm signifies, 'God in us.'"
MADAME DE STAËL (1766–1817), FRANCE

511 **All out** "Whatever I have tried to do in life, I have tried with all my heart to do it well."
CHARLES DICKENS (1812–1870), ENGLAND

512 **Find your real job** "The first duty of a human being is to assume the right functional relationship to society – more briefly, to find your real job, and do it."
CHARLOTTE PERKINS GILMAN (1860–1935), USA

513 **Energy** "Let a man be active, let him throw off this load of misery by faith, goodness, concentration and wisdom."
THE DHAMMAPADA

514 **Wholly present** "Do what you are doing now, suffer what you are suffering now."
JEAN-PIERRE DE CAUSSADE (1675–1751), FRANCE

SUFFERING

515 **Two responses** "If there is a cure when trouble comes, what need is there for being sad? And if no cure is to be found, what use is there in sorrow?"

SANTIDEVA (8TH CENTURY), INDIA

516 **Ending suffering** "There is nowhere where there is no birth, no aging, no decay, no rebirth; nevertheless, I do not say an end of suffering cannot be made. For it can be ended here and now."

THE BUDDHA (THE ANUTTARA NIKAYA)

517 **Once is enough** "If a man do wrong, let him not do so again nor take pleasure in it, for sorrow is the outcome of wrong-doing."

THE DHAMMAPADA

518 **The meaning of happiness** "Even a happy life cannot be without a measure of darkness, and the word 'happy' would lose its meaning if it were not balanced by sadness."

CARL JUNG (1875–1961), SWITZERLAND

519 **An opportunity** "Suffering also has its value: through sorrow, pride is driven out and pity felt for those who wander in samsara, evil is drawn back from and goodness seems delightful."
SANTIDEVA (8TH CENTURY), INDIA

520 **Burnt fingers** "Those who permit themselves longings and desires are like a man who walks in the teeth of the wind carrying a torch. Inevitably, his hands will get burned."
THE BUDDHA (THE SUTRA OF 42 SECTIONS)

521 **Classical wisdom**
"*Felix qui potuit rerum cognoscere causas.*
Happy is he who has been able to learn the causes of things."
VIRGIL (70–19BCE), ROME

522   The wrong battle "Those desiring to escape from suffering hasten right toward suffering. With the very desire for happiness, out of delusion they destroy their own happiness as if it were an enemy."

SANTIDEVA (8TH CENTURY), INDIA

523   Trouble in mind "Our minds can be wonderful, but at the same time they can be our very worst enemy. They give us so much trouble. Sometimes I wish the mind were like a set of dentures which we could leave on our bedside table overnight."

SOGYAL RINPOCHE (BORN 1946), TIBET

524   Self-love "To cherish oneself only brings downfall."

TIBETAN PROVERB

525   Never enough "Nothing is enough for the man to whom enough is too little."

EPICURUS (341–270BCE), GREECE

526 **THE ACORN AND THE OAK**

Buddha-nature is inherent in all things – just as an acorn grows into an oak, or a seed grows into a flower, or an embryo becomes a man or a woman. In humans, this applies not only to our external form but also to the spiritual being within. With all sentient beings, just as with seeds and acorns, the conditions can be helpful – we need light, water, air and food. Buddhist practice creates the right conditions for spiritual growth, avoiding the pitfalls that impede us on the path to wholeness.

527 **The garden of compassion** "Grief can be the garden of compassion. If you keep your heart open through everything, your pain can become your greatest ally in your life's search for love and wisdom."

JALAL UD-DIN RUMI (1207–1273), PERSIA

528 **Looking back** "The evil-doer mourns both in this world and the next; he suffers when he sees the result of his misdeeds."

THE DHAMMAPADA

529 **Baptism of fire** "We are healed of a suffering only by experiencing it in full."

MARCEL PROUST (1871–1922), FRANCE

530 **Admonition** "Impermanence is suffering. All beings are impermanent and die. Haven't you heard about the people who died in the past? Haven't you seen any of your relatives die? Don't you notice that we grow old? And still, rather than practising the Dharma, you forget about past grief."

PADMASAMBHAVA (8TH CENTURY), TIBET

531 Anger burns "Those tormented by the pain of anger will never know tranquillity of mind. Strangers to every joy and pleasure, sleep deserts them. They will never rest."
SANTIDEVA (8TH CENTURY), INDIA

532 Casting a shadow "The greater the light, the stronger will be the shadow."
ANNA CORA MOWATT (1819–1870), USA

533 Delayed results "Have patience and endure: this unhappiness will one day be beneficial."
OVID (43BCE–17CE), ROME

534 Herons "Those who have not led a good life and have earned no merit in their youth perish like old herons by a lake with no fish."
THE DHAMMAPADA

535 Bravery "It requires more courage to suffer than to die."
NAPOLEON BUONAPARTE (1769–1821), FRANCE

DELUSION

536 **Widening the circle** "A human being experiences himself, his thoughts and feelings as something separated from the rest. ... This delusion is a kind of prison for us, restricting us to our personal desires and to affection for the few persons nearest to us. Our task must be to free ourselves from this prison by widening our circle of compassion to embrace all living creatures."

ALBERT EINSTEIN (1879–1955),
GERMANY/USA

537 **Wandering far** "Not knowing how near the truth is, people seek it far away – what a pity! They are like one who, in the midst of water, cries pitifully from thirst or like the son of a rich man who wanders away among the poor."

HAKUIN (1685–1768), JAPAN

538 **Self-made** "Each of us literally chooses, by his way of
attending to things, what sort of universe he shall appear
to himself to inhabit."
WILLIAM JAMES (1842–1910), USA

539 **THE BLIND MEN AND THE ELEPHANT**
To illustrate the fact that doctrinal arguments
are based on personal opinions, the Buddha
called for eight blind men to be shown an
elephant. Each man touched part of the
elephant: head, ear, tail, leg, trunk, tusk,
side, and the tuft of the tail. Then each was
asked what an elephant was. The man who
had touched its head declared, "An elephant
is a pot!" Another who had the ear said,
"No, an elephant is a leather flap." Others
asserted that the tail was a brush, the leg
a pillar and so on. Eventually they argued,
unaware of the partiality of their views.

540   Flowers in empty air "The heart itself creates delusion. All pairs of opposites are the product of our own folly. Dreams, delusions, flowers in the empty air – why trouble to take hold of them?"

SOSAN (DIED 606), CHINA, THE THIRD ZEN PATRIARCH

541   The scarecrow "A farmer will set up a scarecrow to protect his seeds and for a time the birds will mistake it for a man. Similarly, sense and mental objects deceive our mind by producing a false impression. The Buddha, therefore, compares perception to a mirage."

PIYADASSI THERA (1914–1998), SRI LANKA

542   Myopia "Every man takes the limits of his own field of vision for the limits of the world."

ARTHUR SCHOPENHAUER (1788–1860), GERMANY

543   Shadow quest "Beware that you do not lose the substance by grasping at the shadow."

AESOP (620–560BCE), GREECE

544 **Limpet** "When a particular perception, perverted or not, occurs frequently, it grows stronger and grips our mind. Then it becomes difficult to get rid of that perception."
PIYADASSI THERA (1914–1998), SRI LANKA

545 **Mirror image** "This world of appearance has, from the very beginning, never come into existence and is like a mirror image. It has no substance, yet it appears to be there. Having seen this, you quickly reach the citadel of sublime non-attachment."
LONGCHENPA
(1308–1363), TIBET

546 **Fame hurts** "Those who hunger for a name that shall long be remembered and do not study the Way strive vainly. Just as burning incense, though others perceive its pleasant smell, burns itself to ashes, so desires bring with them the danger of fire, which can burn up your bodies."

THE BUDDHA (THE SUTRA OF 42 SECTIONS)

547 **Discomfort** "He who clings to sense-perceptions and to viewpoints wrong and false lives wrangling in this world."

PIYADASSI THERA (1914–1998), SRI LANKA

548 **Clear seeing** "What is, is not; what is not, is. Unless you truly have understood this, you must not tarry in what seems. One in all, all in one."

SOSAN (DIED 606), CHINA, THE THIRD ZEN PATRIARCH

549 **Gullible** "First appearances deceive many."

OVID (43BCE–17CE), ROME

550 **Doing good is not enough** "People under delusion accumulate tainted merits but do not tread the Path. They are under the impression that to accumulate merits and to

tread the Path are one and the same
thing. Though their merits for
alms-giving and offerings are
infinite, they do not realize
that the ultimate source of sin
lies within their own mind."

THE SUTRA OF HUI-NENG

551 **Universal** "Delusion produced not one
mischief the less because it is universal."

EDMUND BURKE (1729–1797), ENGLAND

552 **One big mistake** "The fundamental delusion of humanity
is to suppose that I am here and you are out there."

YASUTANI ROSHI (1885–1973), JAPAN

553 **Willing dupes** "Men in general judge more from
appearances than from reality. All men have eyes, but
few have the gift of penetration."

NICCOLÒ MACHIAVELLI (1469–1527), ITALY

NON-ATTACHMENT

554 **Laying aside sorrow** "Peace of mind cannot come from weeping and wailing. On the contrary, this will lead to more suffering and greater pain. The man who cannot leave his sorrow behind him only travels further into pain."

THE NIPATA SUTTA

555 **Essential** "He who would be serene and pure needs but one thing, detachment. "

MEISTER ECKHART (1260–1328), GERMANY

556 **Commoners and kings** "A king too can only wear one pair of garments and similarly take only a certain measure of food to still his hunger; so too he can use only one bed and only one seat."

ASVAGHOSA (80–150), INDIA

557 **Too many needs** "There is no greater calamity than acquisitiveness racing out of control."

LAO TZU (6TH CENTURY BCE), CHINA

MIND AND HEART – non-attachment 216/217

558 The arithmetic of joy "If thou wilt make a man happy, add
not unto his riches but take away from his desires."
EPICURUS (341–270BCE), GREECE

559 A life lesson "We have to learn, in both meditation and in
life, to be free of attachment to the good experiences, and
free of aversion to the negative ones."
SOGYAL RINPOCHE (BORN 1946), TIBET

560 **Rich and poor alike** "The rich person's attachment to his thousand ounces of gold and the poor man's attachment to his needle and thread are equally binding."

PADMASAMBHAVA (8TH CENTURY), TIBET

561 **A beginning** "Stop attachments, coveting, desires, and let go of embarrassment and timidity in doing deeds that increase merit and engage your talent."

SANTIDEVA (8TH CENTURY), INDIA

562 **Wisdom of age** "The longer one lives, the less importance one attaches to things, and also the less importance to importance."

JEAN ROSTAND (1894–1977), FRANCE

563 **Free of intention** "When an archer is shooting for nothing, he has all his skill. If he shoots for a prize of gold, he goes blind or sees two targets. The prize divides him. He still has all his skill, but the need to win drains him of power."

TRADITIONAL BUDDHIST TEACHING

564 ALL THINGS ARE ON FIRE

Shortly after his enlightenment, the Buddha gave a discourse known as the Fire Sermon. It concerned the "fires" of passion that rage inside every human being. He said, "All things are on fire. Pleasant, unpleasant or indifferent sense-impressions are also on fire. And what are they on fire with? The fires of passion, hatred, infatuation, birth, old age, death, sorrow, lamentation, misery, grief and despair." He explained that through effort, awareness and meditation we can escape the dominance of our senses and thereby free ourselves from our passions and escape the cycle of rebirth.

565 Clinging to self

"I gave up sewn clothes and wore a robe, but I noticed one day the cloth was well-woven. So I bought some burlap, but I still throw it elegantly over my shoulder.

I pulled back my sensual longings and now I discover I'm angry a lot. I gave up rage, and now I notice that I'm greedy all day. I worked hard at dissolving the greed, and now I'm proud of myself. When the mind wants to break its link with the world, it still holds on to one thing."

KABIR (1440–1518), INDIA

566   **Wonderland wisdom** "'Unimportant, of course, I meant,' the king hastily said, and went on to himself in an undertone, 'important – unimportant – important –' as if he were trying which words sounded best."

LEWIS CARROLL (1832–1898), ENGLAND

567   **Goodbye to the frame** "Although this body that is the foundation of all frustrations and unhappiness and the great birthplace of the emotions may be decked with clothes, jewelry and flower garlands, or be pleased and gratified with delicious food and drink, finally you have to part with it because it is transitory and fragile."

LONGCHENPA (1308–1363), TIBET

568 **Reduce your claim** "It is advisable to reduce our claim to enjoyment, possession and recognition to a very modest size, because it is striving and struggling for happiness, glory and enjoyment that brings about the great catastrophe."
ARTHUR SCHOPENHAUER (1788–1860), GERMANY

569 **Enduring pain** "There is no detachment where there is no pain. And there is no pain endured without hatred or lying unless detachment is present too."
SIMONE WEIL (1909–1943), FRANCE

570 **Mutable memory** "Cling not to memories or experiences: they are ever-changing."
PHADAMPA SANGYE
(11TH CENTURY), TIBET

571 **All gone!**
"Cut through
deceptiveness. I
have no questions

now; the ground and root
of mind are gone. There is
no prop, no grasping, no certitude,
no 'this is it'. There is continuousness,
uninterruptedness, wideness, overarchingness."
LONGCHENPA (1308–1363), TIBET

572   The soap of the teachings
"For the seasoned practitioner, even
the Dharma must not
become an
attachment.
As an analogy,

to clean a shirt, it is necessary to use soap. However, if the suds are not then rinsed out, the garment will not be truly clean. Similarly, the practitioner's mind will not be fully liberated until he severs attachment to everything, including the Dharma itself."

TRADITIONAL BUDDHIST TEACHING

573 **Wealth damage** "Just as bodily wounds cause untold suffering, so also wealth creates even greater worries. The fewer the necessities, the greater the happiness. Persecutions are less, and there is no fear of enemies and thieves. Praised by all, you stay on the noble path."

LONGCHENPA (1308–1363), TIBET

574 **The self that never was** "As long as I continue to take myself seriously, how can I consider myself a saint? How can I consider myself a contemplative? For the self I bother about does not really exist, never will, never did except in my own imagination."

THOMAS MERTON (1915–1968), USA

575   **The king and his shadow** "Finally obliged to depart, even a king cannot take his wealth and companions along. But wherever he goes or stays, the results of his actions will follow him, inseparable as a shadow."

FROM *TIBETAN FOLK TALES*

576   **Cycle of doors** "When one door of happiness closes, another opens; but often we look so long at the closed door that we do not see the one which has been opened for us."

HELEN KELLER (1880–1968), USA

577   **Just visiting** "In Tibetan, the word for 'body' is *lu*, which means 'something you leave behind', like baggage. Each time we say *lu*, it reminds us that we are only travellers, taking temporary refuge in this life and body."

SOGYAL RINPOCHE (BORN 1946), TIBET

578   **Change of heart** After a long inner struggle, a samurai in medieval Japan deserted his master. According to the warrior code, such an action was deeply dishonourable, but he felt

an overwhelming vocation for the Zen life. He spent years in
a mountain monastery, and then he set out on a pilgrimage.
Before long he encountered a samurai on horseback, who
recognized him. The warrior made to strike the monk down,
but decided that he was unwilling to sully his sword. Instead
he spat in the monk's face. In the simple act of wiping away
the spit, the monk realized what his reaction would have
been to such an insult in former days. Deeply moved, he
turned toward the mountain where he had trained, bowed
and said: "The mountain is the mountain, and the Way is the
same as of old. Verily what has changed is my own heart."

TRADITIONAL ZEN STORY

579   **Let go** "Detachment cannot bring about frustration,
disappointment and mental torment because there is
no clinging to one thing and another, but letting go."

PIYADASSI THERA (1914–1998), SRI LANKA

580   **Perception** "Our life is what our thoughts make it."

MARCUS AURELIUS (121–180), ROME

HAPPINESS

581 **Self-made** "Happiness is not something ready-made. It comes from your own actions."
HIS HOLINESS THE 14TH DALAI LAMA (BORN 1934), TIBET

582 **Ultimate joy** "The greatest happiness you can have is knowing that you do not necessarily require happiness."
WILLIAM SAROYAN (1908–1981), USA

583 **Be good, be happy** "The righteous man is happy in this world and the next. He is happy when he thinks about the good he has done and happier seeing his good path ahead."
THE DHAMMAPADA

584 **Smile effect** "Sometimes your joy is the source of your smile, but sometimes your smile can be the source of your joy."
THICH NHAT HANH (BORN 1926), VIETNAM/FRANCE

585 **In its place** "It is good to train the wandering mind. A mind under control brings great happiness."
THE DHAMMAPADA

586   **The joy of small things** "The happiest people I have known in this world have been the Saints – and, after them, the men and women who get enjoyment from little things."
HUGH WALPOLE (1884–1941), NEW ZEALAND

587   **Happy and sad** "If others are happy, the great sages rejoice. If others are sad, the sages are sad. When others are content, all the sages rejoice."
ATISA (982–1054), TIBET

588   **The breeze of enthusiasm** "Just as cotton is swayed in the direction of the wind's coming and going, so should we surrender ourselves to our enthusiasm, and in this way our powers will thrive."
SANTIDEVA (8TH CENTURY), INDIA

589   **Not me** "I think that all happiness depends on the energy to assume the mask of some other self; that all joyous or creative life is a rebirth as something not oneself."
W.B. YEATS (1865–1939), IRELAND

590   SNOW LION
The mythological snow lion is white with a turquoise mane. It inhabits the mountain ranges of Tibet, leaping from mountain top to mountain top. Snow lions are the animal symbol of Tibet – they appear on the Tibetan flag, and on currency, stamps and official seals. Thought of as cheerful, friendly creatures, they are often depicted playing. However, they also support the thrones of Buddhist deities.

---

591   A fire inside "Find a place inside where there's joy, and the joy will burn out the pain."
JOSEPH CAMPBELL (1904–1987), USA

592   Love it all "When you come right down to it, the secret of having it all is loving it all."
DR JOYCE BROTHERS (BORN 1925), USA

593 **Living in joy** "Find ecstasy in life; the mere sense of living is joy enough."
EMILY DICKINSON (1830–1886), USA

594 **Pressed for time** "We haven't time to be ourselves. All we have time for is happiness."
ALBERT CAMUS (1913–1960), FRANCE

595 **By the way** "Happiness is not a goal; it is a by-product."
ELEANOR ROOSEVELT (1884–1962), USA

596 **Law-abiding** "He who loves the law lives happily, with his mind at ease. It is good to know such a man."
THE DHAMMAPADA

597 **Joy does it** "One joy scatters a hundred griefs."
CHINESE PROVERB

598 **Desert spring** "If an Arab in the desert were suddenly to discover a spring in his tent, and so would always be able to have water in abundance, how fortunate he would consider himself – so too when a man, who as a physical being is always turned toward the outside, thinking that his happiness lies outside him, finally turns inward and discovers that the source is within."

SØREN KIERKEGAARD (1813–1855), DENMARK

599 Doors of bliss "If you ... follow your bliss, you put yourself on a kind of track that has been there all the while, waiting for you, and the life that you ought to be living is the one you are living."

JOSEPH CAMPBELL (1904–1987), USA

600 Either way "If you want others to be happy, practise compassion. If you want to be happy, practise compassion."

HIS HOLINESS THE 14TH DALAI LAMA (BORN 1934), TIBET

601 Ideal joy "Happiness is not an ideal of reason but of imagination."

IMMANUEL KANT (1724–1804), GERMANY

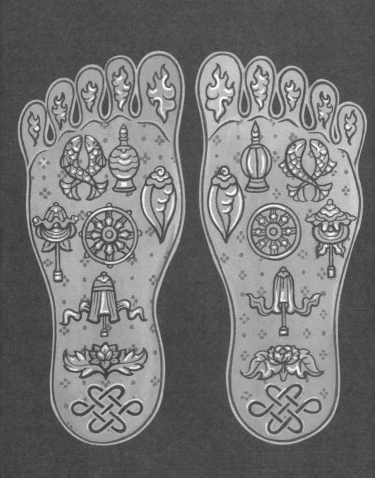

Finding
the path

ASPIRATION

602   **Every human heart** "There is not a heart but has its moments of longing, yearning for something better, nobler, holier than it knows now."

HENRY WARD BEECHER (1813–1887), USA

603   **The meeting with Dipamkara** Legend tells us that Siddhartha, in an earlier birth as a young brahmin, saw the previous Buddha, Dipamkara. Siddhartha begged flowers and offered them in full prostration, with his hair spread upon the ground for Dipamkara to walk on, and vowed to strive on until he too, in a future life, became a Buddha. Dipamkara confirmed that indeed this would happen. This legend demonstrates *bodhicitta*, the aspiration toward enlightenment. To pay tribute and aspire to such an ideal as Buddhahood as greater than oneself will always bear fruit, even in another life.

604   **First step** "A thousand-mile journey begins with a single step."

LAO TZU (6TH CENTURY BCE), CHINA

605 **A new attempt** "A man may fulfil the object of his
existence by asking a question he cannot answer, and
attempting a task he cannot achieve."
OLIVER WENDELL HOLMES (1809–1894), USA

---

606 **THE SPIRIT OF AWAKENING**
Normally we crave for all manner of things,
objects or people to fill our emptiness and
banish our loneliness. This longing for "things",
the source of materialism, is in fact part of
the delusion of "I". When we really examine
it, we realize that we are in fact searching for
something quite different – fulfilment. This
search, this universal longing for the heart's
desire, is a spiritual principle cultivated in
Buddhism. It is called *bodhicitta*. This is may
also be translated as the spirit of awakening,
the enlightenment thought, the longing for
God, or the search for union.

607 **Toward a myriad joys** "Those who long to overcome the abundant miseries of mundane existence, those who wish to dispel the adversaries of sentient beings, and those who yearn to experience a myriad joys should never forsake the spirit of awakening."

SANTIDEVA (8TH CENTURY), INDIA

608 **Far away longing**
"...The desire of the moth for the star,
Of the night for the morrow,
The devotion to something afar
From the sphere of our sorrow."

PERCY BYSSHE SHELLEY (1792–1822), ENGLAND

609 **Ambitious heart** "Do not become conceited just because
you happen to be somewhat quick and clever; the clever
ones need all the more to rely on their heart's aspiration.
And if you deem yourself stupid and dull, unable to keep
up with most people, rely still more upon this aspiration of
the heart. Never be content with small attainment but still
more rely on this aspiration in the heart."

TOREI ENJI ZENJI (1721–1792), JAPAN

610 **Means to enlightenment** "In this
existence there is no other means than
bodhicitta for the realization of our
own and others' benefit. The Buddhas
have until now seen no means apart
from *bodhicitta*."

NAGARJUNA (c.150–250), INDIA

611 **Positive searching** "What we see depends mainly on what
we look for."

JOHN LUBBOCK (1834–1914), ENGLAND

612 **The four great vows** In Mahayana Buddhism, monks take the four vows (given below **613-616**), promising that they will not realize or attain nirvana until all sentient beings are free of the cycle of rebirth. Lay Buddhists also take these vows to assist their spiritual practice.

613 **The first vow** "Sentient beings are innumerable; I vow to liberate them all."

614 **The second vow** "My faults are innumerable; I vow to work through them all."

615 **The third vow** "The teachings are innumerable; I vow to practise them all."

616 **The fourth vow** "The way of the Buddha is unsurpassable; I vow to tread it to the end."

617 **A mist of vows** "Reciting the Four Great Vows and holding them in your heart, chanting them and pondering them day and night, then you will without fail attain the Buddha-Dharma of the Zen way – just as when walking in fine mist our clothes nevertheless get soaking wet, or as the scent of burning incense clings to and perfumes other things as well."

TOREI ENJI ZENJI (1721–1792), JAPAN

618 **A great challenge** "It is all very well talking about Buddhism, BUT CAN YOU DO IT?"

CHRISTMAS HUMPHREYS (1901–1983), ENGLAND

619 **Looking up** "Far away there in the sunshine are my highest aspirations. I may not reach them, but I can look up and see their beauty, believe in them and try to follow where they lead."

LOUISA MAY ALCOTT (1832–1888), USA

620 **Personal progress** "We know who we are, but know not what we may be."
WILLIAM SHAKESPEARE (1564–1616), ENGLAND; FROM *HAMLET*

621 **A vastness of merit** "Simply by generating *bodhicitta*, a mass of merit is collected. If it took form, it would more than fill the expanse of space."
NAGARJUNA (c.150–250), INDIA

622 **Trusty steed** "Mounting the steed of the awakening thought, and spurring it on with the whip of awareness of death, we swiftly traverse the Path – through the region of great fear on life's road – and arrive at the level of fearless Buddhahood."
ATISA (982–1054), TIBET

623 **On the way** "A man protesting against error is on the way towards uniting himself with all men that believe in truth."
THOMAS CARLYLE (1795–1881), SCOTLAND

624 **A clear path** "To have his path made clear for him is the aspiration of every human being in our beclouded and tempestuous existence."
JOSEPH CONRAD (1857–1924), POLAND/ENGLAND

625 **Virtue's ally** "Virtue is perpetually ever so feeble, while the power of vice is great and extremely dreadful. If there were no spirit of perfect awakening, what other virtue would overcome it?"
SANTIDEVA (8TH CENTURY), INDIA

626 **As sparks fly upward** "It is not for man to rest in absolute contentment. He is born to hopes and aspirations as the sparks fly upward, unless he has brutified his nature and quenched the spirit of immortality which is his portion."
ROBERT SOUTHEY (1774–1823), ENGLAND

627 **A solid possession** "An aspiration is a joy forever, a possession as solid as a landed estate."
ROBERT LOUIS STEVENSON (1850–1894), SCOTLAND

LEARNING

628 **With fresh ears** "When reading a sacred text, the eye races over well-known phrases and much may be missed. A hearing may be worth a hundred readings. Record the main texts and play them every morning. Clara Schumann played the Chopin study in C sharp minor every morning for 18 years and found new depths in it. It can be the same with the sacred texts."

TREVOR LEGGETT (1914–2000), ENGLAND

629 **Sucked down** "Vanity is the quicksand of reason."

GEORGE SAND (1804–1878), FRANCE

630 **Cutting through** "Learning doesn't just mean to receive teachings; it means to cut through misconceptions and have realizations beyond conceptual mind."

PADMASAMBHAVA (8TH CENTURY), TIBET

631 **Learning for all** "Consider that I laboured not for myself only, but for all those that seek learning."

THE BOOK OF SIRACH 33:17

632 **Don't stop** "He who adds not to his learning, diminishes it."
THE TALMUD

633 **Voyage of discovery** "All truths are easy to understand once they are discovered; the point is to discover them."
GALILEO GALILEI (1564–1642), ITALY

634 **Total immersion** A master once described the journey to enlightenment as "like filling a sieve with water". When a woman questioned this master on his meaning, he gave her a sieve and a cup, and they went to the sea, where he asked her to fill the sieve with water. She poured a cupful of water into the sieve. It was instantly gone. "Spiritual practice is the same," the master explained, "if we stand on the rock of 'I', and try to ladle the divine realization in. That's not the way to fill the sieve with water, nor the self with divine life."
He took the sieve and threw it into the sea, where it sank. "Now it's full of water, and will remain so. That's spiritual practice. It is not ladling little cupfuls into the individuality, but becoming totally immersed in the sea of divine life."

635 **Like the sun** "Just as the sun ... brings the lotuses to full
bloom, so do the Buddha's sublime teachings ... pour into
the lotuses of beings training in virtue."

JE GAMPOPA (1079–1153), TIBET

636 **Rules of admission** "He who wishes to enter into
Mahayana's door calms his desire, brightening its darkness
with the sun-like and moon-like thought of awakening."
ATISA (982–1054), TIBET

637   **Study and practice** "Alas, few who study Buddhism really want to practise. I certainly urge them to practise, but some people can only study in a logical way. Few are willing to die and be reborn again free. I feel sorry for the rest."

AJAHN CHAH (1918–1981), THAILAND

638   **Beyond category** "The question has often been asked, is Buddhism a religion or a philosophy? It does not matter what you call it. Buddhism is what it is whatever the label you may put on it. The label is immaterial."

WALPOLA RAHULA (1907–1997), SRI LANKA

639   **The four reliances** "Rely on the message of the teacher, not his personality; rely on the meaning, not just the words; rely on the real meaning, not the provisional one; rely on your wisdom mind, not just your ordinary, judgmental mind."

THE BUDDHA (THE HEART SUTRA)

640 **THE OLDEST UNIVERSITY**
Buddhism was introduced into Tibet some
1,200 years ago. The first lamas were Indians
and Tibetans who had studied at northern
India's great Nalanda University, probably
the oldest university in the world. The system
of instruction devised at Nalanda in the early
centuries CE was preserved in Tibet. Until
the Chinese occupation in 1950, the courses
given at Lhasa's monastic universities in such
subjects as metaphysics, astrology, grammar,
logic and medicine, as well as the manner
of student debating, had remained much
the same as they had been at Nalanda, 12
centuries earlier.

641 **Young and old** "Learning is ever in the freshness of its youth,
even for the old."
AESCHYLUS (c.525–456BCE), GREECE

642   The virtuous student "If you have a bad character, you have to do a lot of study. If you have a bad character and try to do good, what you do will usually be disastrous. If you study the texts, it will at least keep you out of mischief, which is a great advantage for the world!"

TREVOR LEGGETT (1914–2000), ENGLAND

643   Unlearning "The most useful piece of learning for the uses of life is to unlearn what is untrue."

ANTISTHENES (444–365BCE), GREECE

644   Pondering "Learning without thought is work lost."

CONFUCIUS (551–479), CHINA

645   Buddhas and masters "In my tradition we revere the masters for being even kinder than the Buddhas themselves. We cannot meet the Buddhas face to face. But we can meet the masters; they are here, living, breathing, speaking and acting to show us the way to liberation."

SOGYAL RINPOCHE (BORN 1946), TIBET

646 **Teacher's lesson** "By learning you will teach, by teaching
you will learn."
LATIN PROVERB

647 **Wind in our sail** "The breeze of divine grace is blowing
upon us all. But we need to set the sail to feel this breeze."
ATTRIBUTED TO RAMAKRISHNA (1836–1886), INDIA

648 **Not just words** "It is a great misfortune for those engaged
in learning to take the sayings of the sages as mere verbal
exercises."
WU-MEN (13TH CENTURY), CHINA

649 **Evil disguised** "If you are not learned but pretend to know,
it is evil. If you are learned but hide it, it is evil."
TIBETAN PROVERB

THE LESSONS OF EXPERIENCE

650   A speck of dust "Once there was a wise man. He saw that the Flower Garland Sutra was contained in a speck of dust, but thus contained, was of little use to sentient beings. He decided, 'With the strength of my devotion I will crack open this particle of dust and extract the *sutra*.' Devising skilful means to do so, he split the mote of dust, extracted the *sutra*, and made it available. What applies to one particle of dust, applies to all dust particles – it applies to everything."

TOREI ENJI ZENJI (1721–1792), JAPAN

651   You don't lose "To change your mind and to follow him who sets you right is to be nonetheless the free agent that you were before."

MARCUS AURELIUS (121–180), ROME

652   Simple faith "When I do good, I feel good. When I do bad, I feel bad. And that is my religion."

ABRAHAM LINCOLN (1809–1865), USA

653 **Runaway donkey** "The spirit and the body carry different loads and require different attentions. Too often we put saddlebags on Jesus and let the donkey run loose."
JALAL UD-DIN RUMI (1207–1273), PERSIA

654 **The way** "Buddhahood, enlightenment, cannot be communicated, but only the way to enlightenment."
JOSEPH CAMPBELL (1904–1987), USA

655 **Four things to avoid** "Four things weaken the thought of enlightenment: deceiving your teacher and others worthy of respect; making others feel guilty for no reason; defaming or disparaging a person who has entered the Mahayana; approaching a friend in guile and deceit."
ATISA (982–1054), TIBET

656 **Understanding needed** "Where there is understanding no comment is needed, but where there's no understanding no amount of argument is convincing."
D.T. SUZUKI (1870–1966), JAPAN

657 **Indirect route** "The treasures of the house do not come in by the front door."
MUMON (1183–1260), CHINA

658 **Age before youth** "Better than the young man's knowledge is the old man's experience."
TIBETAN PROVERB

659 **Three adversaries** "My favourite enemy, the one most easily influenced for good, is the British empire. My second enemy, the Indian people, is far more difficult. But by far my most formidable opponent is a man named Mohandas K. Gandhi. With him I seem to have very little influence."
MAHATMA (MOHANDAS K.) GANDHI (1869–1948), INDIA

660 **Keep your counsel** "Talk doesn't cook rice."
CHINESE PROVERB

661 **Aging gracefully** "Take kindly the counsel of the years, gracefully surrendering the things of youth."

MAX EHRMANN (1872–1945), USA

662 **Mind is moving** A Zen story tells of two monks, who were watching a flag blow in the wind. One monk said, "The flag is moving." The other monk said, "No, the wind is moving." A Zen master happened to be passing by, and he told them, "Not the wind, nor the flag; the mind is moving."

663 **Choose your companions** "Live with wolves, and you learn to howl."

SPANISH PROVERB

664 **The three ages of man** "In childhood be modest, in youth temperate, in adulthood just, and in old age prudent."

SOCRATES (470–399BCE), GREECE

665 **Two Lamas** There are two main spiritual leaders of Tibetan Buddhism. The Dalai Lama, Buddha's vice-regent on earth, deals with the temporal and spiritual affairs of this world. The Panchen Lama is concerned with the other world, passing his days in communication with Heaven.

666 **Many lives, one vow** The Indian monk Santideva wrote: "As long as space endures and sentient beings remain, may I remain and dispel the miseries of the world." The 14th Dalai Lama has said of this vow: "I make this wish in my present life and I am sure I made it in past lives too."

667 **Gentle spirits** An *apsara* is a female spirit of the clouds and waters. They appear in Hindu as well as Buddhist mythology. This *apsara* (illustrated) carries a conch shell, symbol of the deep and beautiful sound of the teachings of the Dharma (see page 261).

DEVOTION

668   **A true follower** "The man who can repeat but little of the teaching yet lives it himself, who forsakes craving, hatred and delusion, clings to nothing in this or any other world – he is a follower of the Blessed One."
THE DHAMMAPADA

669   **The holy life** "The purpose of the holy life does not consist in acquiring recognition, or fame, nor in gaining morality, or concentration. The unshakeable deliverance of the heart is the object of the holy life; that is its essence, that is its goal."
THE SAMYUTTA NIKAYA

670   **Open-eyed belief** "Buddhism is not strictly a religion in the sense in which that word is commonly understood, for it is not a system of faith and worship owing any allegiance to a supernatural god. Buddhism does not demand blind faith."
NARADA THERA (1898–1983), SRI LANKA

671   **To heaven** "Devotion, like fire, goeth upward."
ZOROASTER (6TH CENTURY BCE), PERSIA

672   **Inner temple** "There is no need for temples, no need for complicated philosophies. My brain and my heart are my temples; my philosophy is kindness."
HIS HOLINESS THE 14TH DALAI LAMA (BORN 1934), TIBET

673   **True service** "Real love of God does not consist in tear-shedding, nor in that sweetness and tenderness for which usually we long, just because they console us, but in serving God in justice, fortitude and humility."
ST TERESA OF AVILA (1515–1582), SPAIN

674   **In the scales** "Whatever offerings a man may make to gain merit are not worth a small part of reverence."
THE DHAMMAPADA

675   **Prayer wheels** Tibetan Buddhists believe that saying the
mantra "Om Mani Padme Hum" (shown below in Tibetan),
out loud or silently, invokes the powerful benevolent attention
of Avalokiteshvara (see page 190). Spinning the mantra's
written form inside a wheel is also effective. Rolls of paper,
imprinted with many copies of the mantra, are wound around
an axle inside a container, and spun. Viewing a written mantra
is said to have the same effect.

676   **For our sake** "It is for the sake of man, not of God, that
worship and prayers are required; not that God may be
rendered more glorious, but that man may be made better."
HUGH BLAIR (1718–1809), ENGLAND

677   **Six syllables** "When you say the first syllable, Om, it is blessed
to help you achieve perfection in the practice of generosity,
Ma helps the practice of pure ethics, and Ni helps the practice
of tolerance and patience. Pad, the fourth syllable, helps
perseverance, Me helps concentration, and the sixth syllable,
Hum, helps the practice of wisdom."
GEN RINPOCHE (1921–1995), TIBET

678   **Silent journey** "When the soul is in quietness it arises and
leaves the body, and reaching the Supreme Spirit finds there
its body of light. This is the land of infinite liberty where,
beyond its mortal body, the spirit of man is free."
THE UPANISHADS

679   **Objects of devotion** The eight auspicious symbols (illustrated
over the following pages) are popular in Tibetan Buddhism.
They are mentioned in texts dating back to the establishment
of Buddhism in India. In some texts they are compared to
the body, speech and mind of the Buddha. They can also
symbolize aspects of the Dharma.

680 **The parasol** In ancient India and Tibet, important religious dignitaries and secular rulers often walked under silk parasols or ones constructed out of peacock feathers. The parasol symbolizes protection against the heat of defilements.

681 **The wheel** Symbolizing the wheel of Dharma set in motion by the Buddha with his first sermon, the wheel represents the Buddha's teaching. The eight spokes represent the Noble Eightfold Path.

682   **The right-turning conch shell** In Tibetan Buddhism shells
or conches are used to call together an assembly. The conch
stands for the fame of the Buddha's teaching, which spreads
in all directions like the sound of a conch shell trumpet.

683   **The victory banner** This is the sign of victory over all
obstacles – negativity, disagreements, disharmonies – and
the victory of the Buddhist teaching, the triumph of
knowledge over ignorance and the attainment of happiness.

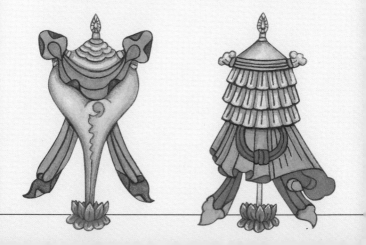

684 **The endless knot** The knot has no beginning and no end. It symbolizes the infinite knowledge of the Buddha and the union of method and wisdom, which at liberation become great compassion and wisdom.

685 **The lotus** This flower is a symbol of mental purity and divine origination. In full bloom it is the image of correct activities leading to liberation. Each plant has its roots in the muddy water of a pond or lake, but beautiful, pristine flowers surrounded by leaves appear above the water.

686   **The treasure vase** The vase is a sign of abundance and the
fulfilment of spiritual and material wishes. Treasure vases are
also an attribute of particular deities connected with wealth
of one kind or another.

687   **The golden fishes** The fishes symbolize the fearless life and
knowing how to avoid falling into the ocean of suffering
and samsara. They have all the freedom and liveliness of
fish swimming and leaping from the water. They originally
represented the sacred rivers Ganges and Yamuna.

688   The heart of the believer

On his journey home from a long pilgrimage, a young man recalled that he had promised to bring back a holy relic for his mother. "My old mother is so superstitious," he said to himself, "A bit of bone will do." He broke off a tooth from a dog's skeleton, wiped it clean, and gave it to his mother, telling her it was a relic. Overjoyed, she worshipped before the tooth daily, while her son smiled behind her back. However, one day he was amazed to find brilliant rays emanating from the shrine: the tooth had transformed into a true holy relic. From this story comes the saying, "Sincere prayer, worship and supplication can make even a thorn a relic of adoration."

TRADITIONAL TIBETAN BUDDHIST STORY

689   Soul's language "Prayer is not asking. It is a language of the soul."

MAHATMA GANDHI (1869–1948), INDIA

690   **True servant** "The worth of love does not consist in high feelings but in detachment, in patience under trials for the sake of the god whom we love."
ST JOHN OF THE CROSS (1542–1591), SPAIN

691   **Buddhist devotion** "Religion as propounded by the Buddha is startlingly different from all other great religions. Devotion to the Dharma, and loving service, take the place of worship. ... Becoming morally perfect and living a good life take the place of rituals and ceremonies."
P.D. MEHTA (1902–1994), INDIA

692   **Humility** "All is holy where devotion kneels."
OLIVER WENDELL HOLMES (1809–1894), USA

693   **The best prayer**
"He prayeth best, who loveth best
All things, both great and small."
SAMUEL TAYLOR COLERIDGE
(1722–1834), ENGLAND

GRATITUDE

694 **Just two words** "If the only prayer you ever said in your life was 'thank you', that would suffice."
MEISTER ECKHART (1260–1328), GERMANY

695 **Take nothing for granted** "Developing a true sense of gratitude involves taking absolutely nothing for granted. Rather, we always look for the friendly intention behind the deed and learn to appreciate it."
ALBERT SCHWEITZER (1875–1965), FRANCE/GABON

696 **Inner fault** "If you see no reason for giving thanks, the fault lies in yourself."
NATIVE AMERICAN PROVERB

697 **Homage to a saint** "Though month after month with a thousand coins we should make an offering for a hundred years, yet, if only for a moment we should pay homage to a saint who has perfected himself, that homage is, indeed, better than a century of sacrifice."
THE DHAMMAPADA

698   **Song of joy** "All is beautiful, all is more beautiful, and life is thankfulness."
IGUILIK ESKIMO SONG

699   **The heart's blossom** "Gratitude is the fairest blossom which springs from the soul."
HENRY WARD BEECHER (1813–1887), USA

700   **A Buddhist prayer** "Imaginatively, I make an offering to the Buddha, with as many atoms as there are in the world, and with all the wealth in all the millions of worlds."
LONGCHENPA (1308–1363), TIBET

701   **Unfamiliar** "I feel a very unusual sensation … if it is not indigestion, I think it must be gratitude."
BENJAMIN DISRAELI (1804–1881), ENGLAND

702   **Silent thanks** "Be silent as to services you have rendered, but speak of favours you have received."
SENECA (5BCE–65CE), ROME

703 **Peacock feathers** Unlike in the Western tradition, where it suggests vanity, in Tibetan Buddhism the peacock feather is a mystical symbol of good. The bird represents wisdom and love, and its feathers are used to sprinkle holy water.

704 **The grateful parrot** The future Buddha was born as Mahasuka, a parrot who lived in a fig tree whose fruit fed him all year long. The god Saka decided to test him, and caused the tree to wither away. The parrot perched on the stump, unperturbed. Saka asked the parrot why he did not fly away. The parrot replied that he could not desert an old friend who had given him so much. On hearing these words, Saka offered him a boon. The parrot asked for his tree to live again, and it sprang back to life.
THE MAHASUKA JATAKA

705 **Virtue's parent** "Gratitude is not only the greatest of virtues, but the parent of all the others."
CICERO (106–43BCE), ROME

THE MIDDLE WAY

706 **Walking the way** "To walk the Middle Way is to say a big 'yes' to life, to the good as well as the bad, to good fortune as well as ill. It is to walk right down the middle, facing up to suffering and all, without avoiding anything that life brings or being carried away by success or failure, praise or blame, suffering or pleasure."

THE MIDDLE WAY (JOURNAL OF THE BUDDHIST SOCIETY)

707 **Always there** "It is a great joy to realize that the path to freedom which all the Buddhas have trodden is ever-existent, ever-unchanged and ever-open."

JE GAMPOPA (1079–1153), TIBET

708 **Golden mean** "The moral and philosophical system expounded by the Buddha demands no blind faith from its adherents, expounds no dogmatic creeds, encourages no superstitions, rites or ceremonies but advocates a golden mean that guides a disciple through pure thinking and deliverance from evil."

NARADA THERA (1898–1983), SRI LANKA

709 **Going straight ahead** "If a man wants to know the taste of sea water, he has only to set off and go straight ahead. If he keeps going, he is sure to come to the sea. Dipping his finger into it and licking off the drops, at that moment he knows for himself the taste of all the seven oceans."
HAKUIN (1685–1768), JAPAN

710 **Follow the radiance** "When there is neither hate nor lust, the Great Way shines forth in full radiance. If you want to behold it, cease from having opinions about it."
SOSAN (DIED 606), CHINA, THE THIRD ZEN PATRIARCH

711 **Substance and function** "Complete, tranquil, open. Such is the substance of the Way. Expanding, contracting, killing, giving life. Such is its subtle function."
YUAN-WU (1063–1135), CHINA

712 **The sweet spot** "The choicest pleasures of life lie within the ring of moderation."
MARTIN TUPPER (1810–1889), ENGLAND

713   **A silken thread** "Moderation is the silken thread running through the pearl chain of all virtues."
JOSEPH HALL (1574–1656), ENGLAND

714   **Subdue to conquer** "Subdue your appetites, my dears, and you've conquered human nature."
CHARLES DICKENS (1812–1870), ENGLAND;
FROM *NICHOLAS NICKLEBY*

715   **Man's homecoming** "The function of grace is to condition man's homecoming to the centre itself ... which provides the incentive to start on the way and the energy to face and overcome its many and various obstacles."
MARCO PALLIS (1895–1990), ENGLAND

716   **The essence of the way** "Nothing in excess."
SOLON (638–558BCE), GREECE

717   **Spot on** "Going beyond is as bad as falling short."
CHINESE PROVERB

718   **The elephant** Appearing frequently in both Northern and
       Southern traditions, the elephant is said to represent strength
       of mind, noble gentleness, calm majesty, boundless power,
       miraculous aspiration, analysis, intention, and effort. The
       path of the *bodhisattva* has been compared to an elephant
       crossing a river. Neither swimming on the surface nor being
       swept downstream, the elephant crosses the middle of the
       river in a straight line, with its feet on the ground. Unmoved
       by the current, it calmly completes its crossing. This image
       symbolizes the might and majesty of the
       Middle Way.

719 **Fire-proof** "Those who follow the Way are like straw which must be preserved from fire. A follower of the Way who experiences desire must put a distance between himself and the object of that desire."

THE BUDDHA (THE SUTRA OF 42 SECTIONS)

720 **The great heart** "The heart is great that shows moderation in the midst of prosperity."

SENECA (54BCE–39CE), ROME

721 **Wise ones** "Those who have the smallest grain of wisdom would want to walk the simple path of the Great Way. Their only fear would be to go astray."

LAO TZU (6TH CENTURY BCE), CHINA

722   **Eternal light** "Use the light of understanding and the culture of conduct to illuminate and guard your path through life's tunnel of darkness and dismay."
PIYADASSI THERA (1914–1998), SRI LANKA

723   **Truth and illusion** "Those who mistake the shadow for the substance, and the substance for the shadow, never arrive at reality, but follow false aims."
THE DHAMMAPADA

724   **Straying from the path** "If health and a fair day smile upon me, I am a very good fellow. If a corn troubles my toe, I am sullen, out of humour, and inaccessible."
MICHEL DE MONTAIGNE (1533–1592), FRANCE

725   **A tranquil path** "The Middle Way means to act without being swayed by liking and loathing, to walk the path that denies nothing, excludes nothing, fights not, but proceeds step by step by step, tranquil, alert and heedful."
THE MIDDLE WAY (JOURNAL OF THE BUDDHIST SOCIETY)

KARMA

726 Result follows action "All that we are is the result of what we have thought: it is founded on our thoughts and made up of our thoughts. If a man acts or speaks with an evil thought, suffering follows him as the wheel follows the hoof of the beast that draws the wagon."

THE DHAMMAPADA

727 ACTION & EMOTION *Karma* literally means "action". In Buddhist teaching, the word implies intentional action: action motivated by emotion. Every intentional action will bear fruit, for good or ill, either positive or negative, at some time, even in a future life. Thus, we carry *karma* as a burden.

728 **The ideal way** "The perfect man does nothing, the sage takes no action."
CHUANG TZU (3RD CENTURY BCE), CHINA

729 **Individual actions** "There is a difference between actions carried out by a group of people jointly, and actions carried out by a single person. In individual cases, the actions of the earlier part of one's life have an effect on the latter part."
HIS HOLINESS THE 14TH DALAI LAMA (BORN 1934), TIBET

730 **Lingering evil** "An evil deed does not curdle suddenly like milk but pursues the fool like a smouldering fire."
THE DHAMMAPADA

731 **A bird of prey** "Usually we forget what we do, and it is only long afterward that the results catch up with us. 'Imagine an eagle,' says Jikm'e Lingpa. 'It is flying, high in the sky. It casts no shadow. Then suddenly it spies its prey and swoops to the ground. As it drops, its menacing shadow appears.'"
SOGYAL RINPOCHE (BORN 1946), TIBET

732   **And on and on and on**
"I died as a stone – and I rose again as a plant,
I died as a plant – and I rose again an animal,
Then I died an animal and I was born a man.
So why should I fear? When was I diminished by dying?"
JALAL UD-DIN RUMI (1207–1273), PERSIA

733   **Punishing himself** "The liar's punishment is not that he
is not believed, but that he cannot believe anyone else."
GEORGE BERNARD SHAW (1856–1950), ENGLAND

734   **Suffering selves** "Ye who suffer! Know ye suffer from
yourselves. No one else compels."
EDWIN ARNOLD (1832–1904), ENGLAND; FROM *THE LIGHT OF ASIA*

735   **No escape** "Those who act in evil, selfish ways are followed
by the thought, 'I have done wrong,' and the memory of the
act is stored in *karma* to work out its inevitable retribution in
following lives."
THE LANKAVATARA SUTRA

736 **Drop by drop** "Let no man think lightly of evil: 'It will not touch me.' Drop by drop the pitcher is filled, and little by little the fool is filled with evil. Let not a man think lightly of good: 'It cannot be for me.' Drop by drop the pitcher is filled, and little by little the wise man is filled with merit."
THE DHAMMAPADA

737 **Unavoidable consequence** "Fire may become cold, the wind may be caught by a rope, sun and moon may fall down, but the consequence of *karma* is infallible."
JE GAMPOPA (1079–1153), TIBET

738 **Whirlwind** "For they have sown the wind, and they shall reap the whirlwind."
HOSEA 8:7

739 Determination "Our deeds determine us, as much as we determine our deeds."
GEORGE ELIOT (1819–1880), ENGLAND

740 Fear of ripening "To be virtuous doesn't simply mean to wear yellow robes; it means to fear the ripening of *karma*."
PADMASAMBHAVA (8TH CENTURY), TIBET

741 Everything counts "Whatever we have done in our lives makes us what we are when we die. And everything, absolutely everything, counts."
SOGYAL RINPOCHE (BORN 1946), TIBET

742 Ourselves alone "Who creates *karma*? We ourselves, by what we think, say, do, desire and omit, create *karma*."
HIS HOLINESS THE 14TH DALAI LAMA (BORN 1934), TIBET

743 Harsh masters "Men are not punished for their sins but by them."
ELBERT HUBBARD (1856–1915), USA

744 **Pondering the fruit** "How can those who consider how the fruit of helpful and harmful deeds ripens persist in their selfishness for even a single moment?"
NAGARJUNA (c.150–250), INDIA

745 **Self-reliance** "A Buddhist who is fully convinced of the law of *karma* does not pray to another to be saved, but confidently relies on himself for his own emancipation."
MAHASI SAYADAW (1904–1982), MYANMAR

746 **Regardless** "The consequences of our actions take hold of us quite indifferent to our claim that meanwhile we have 'improved'."
FRIEDRICH NIETZSCHE (1844–1900), GERMANY

747 **Taking responsibility** "I am the owner of my *karma*, heir to my actions, born of my actions, related through my actions and have my actions as my arbiter. Whatever I do, for good or for evil, to that will I fall heir …"
THE BUDDHA (THE ANGUTTARA NIKAYA)

748 **Seeds and harvest** "As men think, so they are, both here and hereafter, thoughts being the parent of all actions, good and bad. As the sowing has been, so will the harvest be."
THE TIBETAN BOOK OF THE DEAD

749 **The wise man** "Because this life does not last long – like a dewdrop on a blade of grass – the wise man does not become involved in sin, whose only result is suffering."
ATISA (982–1054), TIBET

750 **Involuntary actions** "*Karma* is all moral and immoral volition and intentional action, mental, verbal and physical. Involuntary and unintentional actions are karmically neutral because volition is not present."
NARADA THERA (1898–1983), SRI LANKA

751 **Extremes** "Throw moderation to the winds, and the greatest pleasures bring the greatest pains."
DEMOCRITUS (460–370BCE), GREECE

BUDDHA-NATURE

752   **Enlightened participation** "The idea of the *bodhisattva* is the one who out of his realization of transcendence participates in the world."

JOSEPH CAMPBELL (1904–1987), USA

753   **Water and ice** "All beings are from the very beginning Buddhas. It is like water and ice: apart from water, no ice. Outside living beings, no Buddhas."

HAKUIN (1685–1768), JAPAN

754   **Endless radiance** "The sun shines by day and the moon shines by night. The brahmin shines in meditation. But the Buddha is radiant by day and by night."

THE DHAMMAPADA

755   **A true brahmin** "He who meditates, does his duty and is rid of evil habits is indeed a brahmin."

THE DHAMMAPADA

756   The great physician "With mind unbending as the Earth; keen as the diamond, unruffled as the heavens; uncomplaining; yea, a very street-sweeper in his utter humility. His counsel is thine protection, and thine own good deeds the routing of the foe."

FROM *THE WISDOM OF BUDDHISM*

757   True meditation "The true Buddha is in the home; the real Way is everyday life. A man who has sincerity, who is a peace-maker, cheerful in looks and gentle in his words, harmonious in mind and body … such a man is vastly superior to one who practises breathing control and introspection."

HUNG YING-MING (DIED 1596), CHINA

758 **Fountainhead** "This identity, out of the one and into the one and with the one, is the source of and fountainhead and breaking forth of glowing love."

MEISTER ECKHART (1260–1328), GERMANY

759 **A single quality** "If there were one thing that could be placed in the palm of our hand to represent all the Buddha's qualities, what would it be? Great compassion."

JE GAMPOPA (1079–1153), TIBET

760 **Non-duality** "Look hither at the mind that introduces the distinctions. Mind is like the sky, independent of all affirmation and negation; clouds may appear and disappear in the sky, but the sky's magic remains pure. So also it is with primordial Buddhahood, spotless in itself. It is uncreated, spontaneously present meaningfulness."

LONGCHENPA (1308–1363), TIBET

761 **In your own mind** "*Bodhi* [enlightenment] is to be looked for within your own mind. You seek in vain for a solution to the mystery in the outside world."

MATSUO BASHŌ (1644–1694), JAPAN

762 **Immunity** "When we live in complete integrity, we will be innocent like newborn babies. Wasps and scorpions will not sting us, wild beasts will not maul us. Birds of prey will not seize us. ... We'll sing all day long without becoming hoarse because we'll be in full harmony."

LAO TZU (6TH CENTURY BCE), CHINA

763 **A state of mind** "I remembered today that the Brahmin Mohini said, 'When I was young I was happy. I thought truth was something that could be conveyed from one man's mind to another. I now know that it is a state of mind.'"

W.B. YEATS (1865–1939), IRELAND

764 **Growing in the wilderness** "All living beings are the roots of the *bodhi*-tree; all Buddhas and *bodhisattvas* are its flowers and fruits. By benefiting all beings with the water of great compassion, we can realize the flowers and fruits of the Buddha's and *bodhisattvas'* wisdom."

THE AVATAMSAKA SUTRA

765 **The comfortable brahmin** "Even though richly clothed, he who is calm and controlled, and lives a good life and does no harm to others, is a brahmin or *bhikkhu*."

THE DHAMMAPADA

766 **Flight path** "He whose appetites are controlled, who cares little about food, who realizes the unreality of all things – his path is like that of the birds of the air."

THE DHAMMAPADA

767 **This very earth** "How limitless the sky of unbounded freedom! How pure the perfect moonlight of wisdom! This very earth is the lotus-land of purity, and this body ... is the body of the Buddha."
HAKUIN (1685–1768), JAPAN

768 **Humble pilgrim** "Would you become a pilgrim on the road of love? The first condition is that you make yourself humble as dust and ashes."
SHEIKH KHWAJA ABDULLAH ANSARI (1006–1088), PERSIA

769 **Scripture's echo** "The Kingdom of Heaven is within you."
LUKE 17:21

770 **Inside outside** "If the inner mind is not deluded, then outer deeds will not be wrong."
TIBETAN BUDDHIST TEACHING

771 **Inner compass** "There is an inner compass, which will show itself when the mind is brought to complete stillness. When the conditions are right, the inner compass has a life of its own. It directs the mind to the Pole of the cosmic purpose. The meditator comes to know what to do in life and, when facing the right direction, also gets the energy to do it."

TREVOR LEGGETT (1914–2000), ENGLAND

772   A single truth "One nature, perfect and all-pervading, circulates in all natures ... the embodied truth of all the Buddhas enters into my own being, and my own being is found in union with theirs."

YOKA DAISHI (665–713), JAPAN

773   Your choice Meister Eckhart (1260–1328) told the story of two students from the University of Paris, who visited the Catholic mystic John Ruysbroeck in his hermitage. They asked him to furnish them with a short phrase or motto, which might serve them as a rule of life. "*Vos estis tam sancti sicut vultis,*" answered Ruysbroeck. "You are as holy as you will yourself to be."

774 **In accord** "If the heart is in accord with what is, all single strivings have ceased, all doubts are cleared up, true faith is confirmed; nothing remains, nothing need be remembered. Empty, clear, self-illuminating, the heart does not waste its energy."

SOSAN (DIED 606), CHINA, THE THIRD ZEN PATRIARCH

775 **Nurture and protection** "A *bodhisattva* who is most properly nurtured by a good mentor will not fall into the lower states. A *bodhisattva* who is totally protected by a good mentor will not be swayed by corrupting friends."

JE GAMPOPA (1079–1153), TIBET

776 **The way we walk** "The all-important thing is not killing or giving life ... winning or losing. It is how we win, how we lose, how we live or die and, finally, how we choose."

R.H. BLYTH (1898–1964), ENGLAND

NIRVANA

777 **One day** "Better a day with a vision of nirvana than a hundred years of blindness to the truth."

THE DHAMMAPADA

778 **Not separated** "Those who are suffering or who fear suffering think of nirvana as an escape and a recompense. They imagine that nirvana consists in the future annihilation of the senses and mind; they are not aware that universal mind and nirvana are one, and that this life-and-death world and nirvana are not to be separated."

THE LANKAVATARA SUTRA

779 **Released from the cycle** "By not holding to fixed views, the pure-hearted one, having clarity of vision, being freed from all sensual desires, is not born again into this world."

THE METTA SUTTA

780   **The right road** "One is the road that leads to wealth, another
the road that leads to nirvana. The disciple of the Buddha,
therefore, will not wish for the praise of men, but will rather
seek solitude."
THE DHAMMAPADA

781   **Transcendent** "Nirvana is where there is no birth, no
extinction. It is seeing into the state of suchness, absolutely
transcending all the categories constructed by the mind,
for it is the Buddha's inner consciousness."
THE LANKAVATARA SUTRA

782   **Daylight** "Nirvana is not the blowing out of the candle.
It is the extinguishing of the flame because day is come."
RABINDRANATH TAGORE (1861–1941), INDIA

783   **Freedom from concepts** "The cycle of rebirth springs from
conceptual thought, which is its very nature. The complete
removal of such thought is the highest nirvana."
ATISA (982–1054), TIBET

784   Final destination "When the envelopment of consciousness has been annihilated, then we becomes free of all fear, beyond the reach of change, enjoying final nirvana."
THE HEART SUTRA

785   All mind "This mind itself is the continuum of experience as vast as the sky. This sky itself, throughout time, does not step out of itself or turn into something other than itself; this unchangingness is the primordial nirvana. Like the sky, the mind has limpid clearness and consummate perspicacity."
LONGCHENPA (1308–1363), TIBET

786   Wherever you are "Do not sit at home, do not go to the forest but recognize mind wherever you are. When we abide in complete and perfect enlightenment, where are samsara and nirvana?"
FROM *THE WISDOM OF BUDDHISM*

787   No death "There is no death. Only a change of worlds."
CHIEF SEATTLE (1786–1866), USA

788 **Beyond words** "Nirvana is ineffable and incommunicable. In our attempt to explain it we use words which have limited meanings, words connected with the cosmos, whereas nirvana, the absolute reality, which is realized through the highest mental training and wisdom, is beyond any cosmic experience, beyond the reach of speech."

PIYADASSI THERA (1914–1998), SRI LANKA

789 **Infinite** "If the doors of perception were cleansed, everything would appear to man as it is, infinite."

WILLIAM BLAKE (1757–1827), ENGLAND

790 **Breaking shackles** "He is the greatest of men who is not credulous. He who has destroyed the causes of rebirth and broken every bond knows the reality of nirvana."

THE DHAMMAPADA

791 **Forever pure** "It is profound, uncomplicated thatness: lucid and uncreated, it never arose, will never cease and is primordially pure. It is the state, without middle or end, which by its very nature is nirvana. Behold it with the fine eye of mind, undistorted by concept and without the blurs of sluggishness or agitation."

ATISA (982–1054), TIBET

792 **Trial and error** "Liberation is simply the exhaustion of error."

JE GAMPOPA (1079–1153), TIBET

793 **Cut through** "When you reach the point where feelings are ended, views are gone, and your mind is clean and naked, you open up to Zen realization. After that it is also necessary to develop consistency, keeping the mind pure and free at all times. Cut through resolutely, and then your state will be peaceful."

YUAN-WU (1063–1135), CHINA

794 **Inner light** "There is a light that shines beyond all things on Earth, beyond us all, beyond the highest, the very highest heavens. This is the light that shines in our heart."

THE UPANISHADS

Planet and cosmos

TIME

795 **The now** "The past does not exist, the future is nowhere discovered, and how can the present shift from place to place?"
NAGARJUNA (c.150–250), INDIA

796 **A conundrum** "One instant is eternity; eternity is the now. When you see through this one instant, you see through the one who sees."
WU-MEN (13TH CENTURY), CHINA

797 **Seeing forever**
"... To see a world in a grain of sand,
And a heaven in a wild flower,
Hold infinity in the palm of your hand
And eternity in an hour."
WILLIAM BLAKE (1757–1827), ENGLAND

798 **Begin at once** "Self-salvation is for any man the immediate task. If a man is wounded by

a poisoned arrow, he does not delay extraction by
demanding details of the man who shot it or
the length and make of the arrow.
There will be time for ever-increasing
understanding of the teachings
during the treading of the Way."
SAYING OF THE BUDDHA, RETOLD BY
CHRISTMAS HUMPHREYS (1901–1983),
ENGLAND

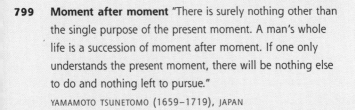

799   Moment after moment "There is surely nothing other than
the single purpose of the present moment. A man's whole
life is a succession of moment after moment. If one only
understands the present moment, there will be nothing else
to do and nothing left to pursue."

YAMAMOTO TSUNETOMO (1659–1719), JAPAN

800   Reincarnation "After all, it is no more surprising to be
born twice than it is to be born once."

VOLTAIRE (1694–1778), FRANCE

801 **Wonderful waking** "Life contains a lot of evils, as fragile as a bubble cast up by a wave, and so how marvellous to wake from sleep still breathing and say, 'I'm awake! There's still time!'"

ATISA (982–1054), TIBET

802 **COSMIC TIME**
The Buddhist unit of measurement of cosmic time is the *kalpa*, a period that is so long it cannot be calculated in years. A period of creation is followed by a period of the duration of creation; this is followed by a period of dissolution and then a period of nothingness. The path of the *bodhisattva* and the attainment of Buddhahood can last for thousands of *kalpa*s, a process of refinement and discipline lasting over hundreds of thousands of rebirths.

803   **Eons** "It was after a very long time, after he had passed through a hundred thousand *kalpa*s in quest of the perfection of enlightenment, that the infinitely precious Buddha appeared in the world."
THE MAHAVASTU

804   **Summer days** "Sweet childish days, that were as long as twenty days are now."
WILLIAM WORDSWORTH (1770–1850), ENGLAND

805   **Immortal presence** "Because God always has an eternal and present state, His knowledge surpasses the concept of time and remains in the simplicity of His presence. Comprehending the infinite whole of what is past and to come, it considers all things as though they were happening at the present time."
BOETHIUS (480–524), ROME

806   **Choose carefully** "Life is very short and many are the kinds of

knowledge; let him who knows not even his own life's span choose only from his purest desires."
ATISA (982–1054), TIBET

807   A pinprick "Every instant of time is a pinprick of eternity."
MARCUS AURELIUS (121–180), ROME

808   The busy bee "Eternity is in love with the productions of time. The busy bee has no time for sorrow. The hours of folly are measured by the clock, but of wisdom, no clock can measure."
WILLIAM BLAKE (1757–1827), ENGLAND

809   Wisdom of the moment "Do not chase after what is passed, do not worry over what is yet to come. The past is already thrown away, the future has not arrived. Simply grasp wholeheartedly what is here and now and without wavering, without yielding, look into it directly

and realize it. Do today what should be done today, simply and mindfully. Nobody knows if death will come tomorrow, and there is no escaping this invincible adversary. Achieve in this instant what must be achieved."

THE MIDDLE WAY (JOURNEY OF THE BUDDHIST SOCIETY)

810 **Fearsome foes** "The two most powerful warriors are patience and time."

LEO TOLSTOY (1828–1910), RUSSIA

811 **No distinction** "People like us, who believe in physics, know that the distinction between past, present and future is only a stubbornly persistent illusion."

ALBERT EINSTEIN (1879–1955), GERMANY/USA

812 **The hourglass** "A person's life is passing with every minute or second; day and night it moves closer to the domain of the Lord of Death, just like the water of a waterfall flowing into the ocean or the sun setting behind the mountain."
LONGCHENPA (1308–1363), TIBET

813 **Time and no time**
"High above us the myriad stars
Glow full as they turn.
Yet in you the outliving of stars
Has already begun."
RAINER MARIA RILKE (1875–1926), GERMANY

814 **Moments are enough** "The butterfly counts not months but moments, and has time enough."
RABINDRANATH TAGORE (1861–1941), INDIA

815 **Knowing the value** "The man who dares to waste one hour of time has not discovered the value of life."
CHARLES DARWIN (1809–1882), ENGLAND

816   **The path not taken** "It is never too late to be what you
might have been."
GEORGE ELIOT (1819–1880), ENGLAND

817   **A time and a season** "For everything there is a season,
and a time for every matter under heaven."
ECCLESIASTES 3:1

818   **The seven ages** "He who thinks to realize the hopes and
desires of his youth when he is older is always deceiving
himself, for every decade of a man's life possesses its own
kind of happiness, its own hopes and prospects."
JOHANN WOLFGANG VON GOETHE (1749–1832), GERMANY

819   **Every instant** "The infinite is in the finite of every instant."
ZEN SAYING

820   **Loving life** "Dost thou love life? Then do not squander time,
for that is the stuff life is made of."
BENJAMIN FRANKLIN (1706–1790), USA

IMPERMANENCE

821   **The miracle of breathing** "There are many things which harm life. As life is more unstable than an air bubble in water, it is a wonder that in-breaths turn into out-breaths and that one wakes up from sleep."

JE GAMPOPA (1079–1153), TIBET

822   **River of life** "All is flux; nothing stays still."

HERACLITUS (c.535–475BCE), GREECE

823   **Changing seasons** "We cling to our own point of view, as though everything depended on it. Yet our opinions have no permanence: like autumn and winter, they gradually pass away."

CHUANG TZU (3RD CENTURY BCE), CHINA

824   **Foam, bubbles, mirage** "Form is like a mass of foam, feeling is like bubbles, apprehension is like a mirage ... consciousness is like an illusion."

NAGARJUNA (c.150–250), INDIA

825 **Lightning flash** "This world is transitory, like an autumnal cloud. The birth and death of beings is like watching a dance. The length of a being's life is like a lightning flash, coming swiftly and abruptly to an end, like water dashing over a steep precipice."
FROM *TIBETAN FOLK TALES*

826 **Peace of knowing** "Many do not realize that all must one day die. In those who know this fact all strife is stilled."
THE DHAMMAPADA

827 **Body lamp** "As this life, like a lamp in the wind, has little certainty of lasting, we must begin in earnest to keep meditation like a flame burning in the head or body."
ATISA (982–1054), TIBET

828 **Gifts of a flame** "This sense of being suspended over nothingness and yet in life, of being a fragile thing, a flame that may blow out and yet burns brightly, adds an inexpressible sweetness to the gift of life, for one sees it entirely and purely as a gift; a gift that one must treasure in great fidelity with a truly pure heart."

THOMAS MERTON (1915–1968), USA

829 **Certain forecast** "What is born will die, what has been gathered will be dispersed, what has been accumulated will be exhausted, what has been built up will collapse and what has been high will be brought low."

SOGYAL RINPOCHE (BORN 1946), TIBET

830 **Last moment** "Indomitable faith combined with supreme serenity of mind are indispensable at the moment of death."

JE GAMPOPA (1079–1153), TIBET

831 **Listen! Listen!**
"Listen,
all creeping things –
the bell of transience."

ISSA (1763–1827), JAPAN

832   **Eternal** "Change alone is eternal, perpetual, immortal."
ARTHUR SCHOPENHAUER (1788–1860), GERMANY

833   **Memento mori** "Someday I'll be a weather-beaten skull
resting on a grass pillow, serenaded by a stray bird or two,
no more enduring than last night's dream."
RYOKAN (1758–1831), JAPAN

834   **Brief candle** "Out, out, brief candle!
Life is but a walking shadow, a poor player ..."
WILLIAM SHAKESPEARE (1564–1616), ENGLAND; FROM *MACBETH*

835   **Even the Buddha** "Even our Lord Buddha demonstrated
impermanence by passing into nirvana."
LONGCHENPA (1308–1363), TIBET

836   **What is life?** "It is a flash of a firefly in the night. It is the
breath of a buffalo in the winter time. It is the little shadow
that runs across the grass and loses itself in the sunset."
CROWFOOT (c.1830–1890), USA

837   Deep changes "The purpose of reflection on death is to make a real change in the depths of our hearts. Often this will require a period of retreat and deep concentration, because only that can truly open our eyes to what we are doing with our lives."
SOGYAL RINPOCHE (BORN 1946), TIBET

838   Ancient city "Quickly engage in the quest for the real meaning of life because everything is impermanent, like a city that has grown old."
LONGCHENPA (1308–1363), TIBET

839   Mountains are molehills "In the presence of eternity, the mountains are as transient as the clouds."
ROBERT GREEN INGERSOLL (1833–1899), USA

840   The mustard seed Kisa Gotami, the wife of a rich man, had a beautiful little boy, whom she utterly adored. One day he fell ill and suddenly died. Kisa Gotami could not accept the reality of his death. She carried his body around in her arms, desperately seeking a cure for his "illness". Eventually she was advised to seek help from the Buddha, whom she begged for medicine to cure her child. The Buddha understood the situation and said, "Ask one of your friends for a single mustard seed." The woman was overjoyed. "But," said the Buddha, "you can accept the seed only from a house where no one has died." Kisa Gotami searched, but no one could help her – in every house, someone had died. Finally she returned to the Buddha, comforted by the understanding that she was not alone, and able to let go and cremate her child. She thanked the Buddha with tears in her eyes, and he accepted her thanks with tears of compassion in his own.

841 **On the stream** "The life of beings is like a bubble in water."
TIBETAN PROVERB

842 **Universal truth** "All things change; nothing perishes."
OVID (43BCE–17CE), ROME

SAMSARA

843   **Crossing the river** "If I make no effort to cross the river of frustration while having the boat of unique occasion and right juncture with its captain the guru's instructions, there is nothing else but for me to be deceived, and to be carried away by this river."

LONGCHENPA (1308–1363), TIBET

844   **The raft of the Dharma** "Few men reach the other shore. The rest run up and down this side of the torrent. But those who follow the Dharma will reach the further shore, and pass through the realm of death which is so hard to cross."

THE DHAMMAPADA

845   **A hair's work** "If all realms throughout the world were to become one huge enclosure of water, and one man worked at dipping the water from it with the tip of a single hair for hundreds of thousands of years, that water might diminish somewhat; but there is no such lessening of the realm of creatures."

ATISA (982–1054), TIBET

846   **THE CYCLE OF REBIRTH**
The word "samsara" comes
from Sanskrit and literally
means "wandering
through". Samsara is the
perpetual cycle of birth,
suffering, old age, death
and rebirth in which those who
have not reached enlightenment are trapped,
and are destined to continue. Ignorant of
the true nature of reality, beings move from
state to state on account of their volitional
actions (*karma*) and thus experience repeated
suffering. The purpose of Buddhist practice
is to break this cycle of suffering.

847   **Moth to a flame** "Although there may be the desire and
intent to find bliss and be free from frustration, frustration
rushes on you, being both cause and effect. You are

deceived by your addiction to and desire for sensuous
objects, as is the moth by the flame of a lamp."

LONGCHENPA (1308–1363), TIBET

848   The mind is master "The world of life and death is
created by mind, is in bondage to mind, is ruled by
mind; and the mind is master of every situation. As the
wheels follow the ox that draws the cart, suffering follows
the mind that surrounds itself with impure thoughts and
worldly possessions."

THE LANKAVATARA SUTRA

849   The wise "As the same
person inhabits the body
through childhood, youth, and
old age, so too at the time of
death he attains another body.
The wise are not deluded by
these changes."

THE BHAGAVAD GITA

850   Miraculous dawn The Buddha compares the human
condition to that of a traveller on a stormy night. Suffering
is like the dark night that surrounds the traveller. The flashes
of lightning are the rare occasions of joy that excite the
human mind (such as a birth or a promotion). Enlightenment
is the dawn, bringing an end to the dark night.

851   Don't wait "Do not wait any longer, but cross over the
ocean of fictitious being and quickly travel to the island of
peace, where you will have passed beyond suffering."
LONGCHENPA (1308–1363), TIBET

852   A dark forest, a lost path
"Midway upon the journey of my life
I found myself in a dark forest.
I had strayed away from the straight path.
Oh! How hard it is to say,
What was this forest savage, rough and stern,
Which as I think of it renews the fear."
DANTE ALIGHIERI (1265–1321), ITALY; FROM *INFERNO*, CANTO 1

853   **Freeing ourselves** "Beings who are full of desire fall back into the stream of craving they have generated, just as a spider is tied to the web it has spun. The wise, cutting off the bond of craving, walk on resolutely, leaving all ills behind."
THE DHAMMAPADA

854   **Distraction** "The heart of the ordinary unenlightened man, because of his surroundings, is always liable to change, just like monkeys jumping from one branch to another."
HONEN BO GENKU (1133–1212), JAPAN

855   **Sit still** "If you chase wildly around, wanting to follow others, even after thousands of years you will only end up by returning to birth and death. Better it is ... crossing one's legs on the meditation cushion, to just sit."
RINZAI (DIED 866), CHINA

856 **Good deeds** "Until the very last rebirth in this beginningless samsara, I will perform endless deeds for the benefit and good of creatures."
ATISA (982–1054), TIBET

857 **Crossing over** "These four types of individuals are to be found in the world: the individual who goes with the flow; the individual who goes against the flow; the individual who stands fast; and the one who has crossed over, gone beyond, who stands on firm ground, the Brahmin."
THE ANUSOTA SUTRA

858 **Lighting the fire** "You remain in samsara through the power of laziness, therefore ignite the fire of the effort of application."
ATISA (982–1054), TIBET

859 **Out of reach** "As long as you're subject to birth and death, you'll never attain enlightenment."
BODHIDHARMA (5TH–6TH CENTURY), INDIA/CHINA

860 **The world of form** "With body and form go feeling, perception, consciousness and all the activities throughout the world. The arising of form and the ceasing of form, everything that has been heard, sensed and known, sought after and reached by the mind – all this is the embodied world."

THE SAMYUTTA NIKAYA

861 **Embracing our potential** "By renouncing samsara, we renounce our habitual, unhappy minds. And by renouncing samsara, we embrace our potential for enlightenment."

LAMA ZOPA RINPOCHE (BORN 1946), TIBET

862 **A despairing search** "Alone in the wilderness, lost in the jungle, the boy is searching, searching! The swelling waters, the far-away mountains and the unending path. Exhausted and in despair he knows not where to go; he only hears the evening cicada singing in the maple woods."

D.T. SUZUKI (1870–1966), JAPAN (VERSES FROM THE BULL-HERDING PICTURES, SEE PAGE 156)

863   The eternal question

"I think about this all through the day, then say to myself at night: Where did I come from? Why am I here? What am I supposed to be doing? I simply don't know. My soul is from somewhere else, I do know that, and I intend to find myself again in this other place."

JALAL UD-DIN RUMI (1207–1273), PERSIA

864   WORLDS OF REBIRTH

There are six kinds of rebirth in samsara: among the gods, fighting demons, hungry ghosts, animals, or humans, or in the hells. Rebirth as a human is seen as an opportunity to develop spiritual awareness. When the Buddha was born, he had been through many rebirths, both human and animal.

NATURE

865 **Snowflakes** "A lacy snowflake glistens in your hand. You can't help looking at it. See how it sparkles in a wonderfully intricate pattern. Then it quivers, melts and lies dead in your hand. It is no more. The snowflake which fluttered down from infinite space on to your hand, where it sparkled and quivered and died – that is yourself. Wherever you see life – that is yourself!"

ALBERT SCHWEITZER (1875–1965), FRANCE/GABON

866 **Unexpected teachers** "We may even derive right instructions from nature, from trees and flowers, from stones and rivers."

PIYADASSI THERA (1914–1998), SRI LANKA

867 **Learning to worship** "The happiest man is he who learns from nature the lesson of worship."

RALPH WALDO EMERSON (1803–1882), USA

868 **The eloquence of offerings** "When a Buddhist offers flowers or lights a lamp before the Buddha image or some sacred object ... these are not acts of worship. ... The flowers soon fade, and the flames that die down speak to him, and tell him of the impermanency of all things."

PIYADASSI THERA (1914–1998), SRI LANKA

869   Zen nature

"In the landscape of spring,
Nothing is better or worse.
The flowering branches grow
Naturally, long or short."

ANCIENT CHINESE POEM

870   Large from small "A huge tree that you can't get your arms around grows from a tiny seedling birth. A tower nine stories high rises from a small heap of earth."

LAO TZU (6TH CENTURY BCE), CHINA

871   Nature's lesson "In nature there are neither rewards nor punishments – there are consequences."

ROBERT GREEN INGERSOLL (1833–1899), USA

872 **THE FLEETING MOMENT**

Haiku, the 3-line poems that began in Japan but are now written all over the world, often take the natural world as their subject. The poems are strongly influenced by the evolution of Zen Buddhism in Japan and its emphasis on the transience of human existence. Thus, haiku often concentrate on the fleeting phenomena of nature, such as dewdrops, butterflies or flowers.

873 Morning glories

"While I intone the sutras,
The morning glories
Are at their best."

KYŌROKU (1655–1715), JAPAN

874 Silent ceremony

"They spoke no word,
The host, the guest
And the white chrysanthemum."

RYOTA (1718–1787), JAPAN

875 Firm belief

"I believe in Buddha,
The green of the ears of the barley,
The absolute truth."

SEISENSUI (1884–1976), JAPAN

876 The key factor "In the case of such global issues as the
conservation of the Earth, and indeed in taking all problems,

the human mind is the key factor. ... Though these issues seem to be beyond anyone's individual capacity, where the problem begins and where the answer must be first sought is within. In order to change the external situation we must first change within ourselves. If we want a beautiful garden, we must first have a blueprint in the imagination, a vision. Then that idea can be implemented and the external garden can be materialized."

HIS HOLINESS THE 14TH DALAI LAMA (BORN 1934), TIBET

877 **Natural enlightenment** "There are many instances where people gained enlightenment by merely watching a leaf fall, the flow of water, a forest fire, the blowing out of a lamp."

PIYADASSI THERA (1914–1998), SRI LANKA

878 **Look down** "In the hope of reaching the moon, men fail to see the flowers that blossom at their feet."

ALBERT SCHWEITZER (1875–1965), FRANCE/GABON

879 Transience
"But pleasures are like poppies spread,
You seize the flower, its bloom is shed,
Or like the snow falls on the river,
A moment white – then melts forever."
ROBERT BURNS (1759–1796), SCOTLAND

880 All is Buddha "Like Indra, the drum, clouds and Brahma,
like the sun and the precious jewel is the Buddha, also like
an echo, like space and like the earth."
JE GAMPOPA (1079–1153), TIBET

881 The web of life "Humankind has not woven the web of life.
We are but one thread within it. Whatever we do to the web,
we do to ourselves. All things are bound together."
CHIEF SEATTLE (1786–1866), USA

882 **The wordless sermon** Toward the end of his life, the Buddha's disciples gathered on Vulture Peak to listen to him preach. He stepped forward, picked a flower and silently showed it to them. Everyone was baffled, except the disciple Mahakasyapa, who smiled. The Buddha said to him, "To you I transmit my Dharma."

883 **The jewel net of Indra** In the heavenly abode of Indra (the Hindu god), there is a wonderful net which stretches out infinitely in all directions. In each eye of the net there is a single, sparkling, multi-faceted jewel. As the net itself is infinite, the jewels are infinite in number. They hang like glittering stars. If we select one of these jewels and look closely at it, we shall discover that in its highly polished surface, every facet of every jewel in the net is reflected. Each jewel reflected in this jewel is also reflected in every other jewel, in an infinite reflecting progression. This image symbolizes the infinitely repeated interrelationship between everything in the cosmos. This relationship is said to be one of simultaneous mutual identity and mutual intercausality.

884 **Longchenpa's offering** In the following four pearls the Tibetan master Longchenpa (see page 172) gives detailed instructions for making an offering to the Buddhas. Many of his visualizations involve natural imagery, which shows the importance of nature to Buddhist devotion. But first, he advises Buddhists to make preparations for setting up the statue of the Buddha and sacred objects "in a pleasant, beautiful and clean place".

885 **Hands and words** "With folded hands in the manner of a lotus flower that is just opening in a lovely pond and with melodious words of praise, let me, devotedly, greet the Buddhas (imagining myself to stand before them) in countless embodiments."

LONGCHENPA (1308–1363), TIBET

886   **Trees and mountains** "I make an offering with jewels, mountains, groves and lotus ponds stirred up by female swans swimming in them, with wish-fulfilling trees from which the sweet fragrance of healing properties drifts forth and which bend under the burden of their flowers and fruits."

LONGCHENPA (1308–1363), TIBET

887   **Lotus and lilies** "I make an offering with the lovely lotus flowers opened by the rays of sun and moon in a cloudless sky and with water lilies having as bracelets bees caught by thousands of shaking leaves."

LONGCHENPA (1308–1363), TIBET

888   **Moon and stars** "I make an offering with the white moon of an autumn night, surrounded by garlands of stars, when it has come out of its eclipse, and with the sun shining in the beauty of its thousand rays, the ornament of the world in the four continents."

LONGCHENPA (1308–1363), TIBET

889 Merry liberty

"Where the bee sucks, there suck I,
In a cowslip's bell I lie,
There I couch when owls do cry,
On the bat's back I do fly.
Merrily, merrily shall I live now
Under the blossom·that hangs on the bough."

WILLIAM SHAKESPEARE (1564–1616), ENGLAND; FROM *THE TEMPEST*

890 Living world "Those who have most power and wealth treat the planet as a thing to be possessed, to be used and abused ... but the planet is a living organism ... and each and every one of us is an inherent part of this very organism."

LAO TZU (6TH CENTURY BCE), CHINA

891 Mountain weather "Climb the mountains and get their good tidings. The winds will blow their own freshness into you, and the storms their energy, while cares will drop off like autumn leaves."

JOHN MUIR (1838–1914), SCOTLAND/USA

892   Natural freedom

"The cloud is free
only to go with the wind.
The rain is free
only in falling.
The water is free only
in its gathering together,
in its downward courses,
in its rising into the air.
In law is rest
if you love the law,
if you enter singing into it
as water in its descent."

WENDELL BERRY (BORN 1934), USA

893   Summer rain

"A frog floating
In the water jar:
Rains of summer."

MASAOKA SHIKI (1867–1902), JAPAN

THE ANIMAL KINGDOM

894 **A scientist's philosophy** "There is a disposition to think that because I am so deeply concerned with the need for reverence for life that my philosophy must be Buddhist, especially in connection with the Buddhist emphasis on the importance of animal life. But there is much more to Buddhism than that; and I hope there may be more to my own philosophy."
ALBERT SCHWEITZER (1875–1965), FRANCE/GABON

895 **Possibilities of rebirth**
"Sea slug, sea slug,
What kind of Buddha
Will you turn into?"
SEISETSU (1871–1917), JAPAN

896 **The deer park** "The lord of Varanasi (Benares) once hunted and killed many deer on his land. The deer king implored him to stop the

unnecessary killing and promised that each day he would give the lord the number of deer he required. One day, he was faced with the necessity of sending a pregnant deer. Rather than sacrifice her with her unborn child, the deer king went to the lord to offer his own flesh instead. The lord was so moved by the deer king's compassion that he stopped the daily killing. Hence the place where all this happened is named the "Deer Park". The deer king was Buddha Shakyamuni in a previous life. His great act of compassion was met by an equally lofty act which resulted in the creation of an animal sanctuary and a pilgrimage site. The Buddha's first sermon was given in this deer park."
HSUAN-TSANG (602–c.664), CHINA

897 **The bird is mine** One day Devadatta, a young cousin of Siddhartha, took a bow and arrow and shot down a swan. The bird was grounded but not killed. The future Buddha took the swan upon his knees and comforted it. Devadatta came to claim

his prize, no doubt intending to kill it, but the Buddha refused to give him the swan, saying that the bird was his. He laid the swan's neck beside his cheek, and gravely said, "Say no! The bird is mine, the first of myriad things that shall be mine, by right of mercy and lord's lordliness."

EDWIN ARNOLD (1832–1904), ENGLAND; FROM *THE LIGHT OF ASIA*

---

898 TIGER, TIGER!

In Buddhism, tigers represent boldness and fearlessness. Like the bull (see page 156), they can also represent the force of the untamed mind. Thus, deities (often "wrathful deities") may be shown riding tigers, or wearing or sitting on tiger skins, and the victory banner is also often decorated with a tiger's skin. The tiger is not native to Tibet – early Tibetan artists and painters would never have seen a tiger, so the animal is sometimes drawn in a very stylized manner.

The global family

SELF AND OTHERS

899   **My happiness, your happiness** "Because our interests
are inextricably linked, we are compelled to accept ethics
as the indispensable interface between my desire to be
happy and yours."
HIS HOLINESS THE 14TH DALAI LAMA (BORN 1934), TIBET

900   **Gentle victories** "Conquer the angry man by love. Conquer
the ill-natured man by goodness. Conquer the miser with
generosity. Conquer the liar with truth."
THE DHAMMAPADA

901   **An echo** "Hurtful expressions should never be used, not
even against an enemy, for inevitably they will return to us,
like an echo from a rock."
JE GAMPOPA (1079–1153), TIBET

902   **Don't criticize** "If you cannot mould yourself entirely as you
would wish, how can you expect other people to be entirely
to your liking?"
THOMAS À KEMPIS (1380–1471), GERMANY

903 **The lucky ones** "Instead of comparing our lot with that of those who are more fortunate, we should compare it with the lot of the great majority of our fellow men."
HELEN KELLER (1880–1968), USA

904 **Cultivate a boundless heart** "It is incumbent on all men of understanding to stop hurting and harming others and to cultivate a boundless heart full of pity and benevolence."
PIYADASSI THERA (1914–1998), SRI LANKA

905 **A greater evil** "Whatever an enemy may do to his enemy, a wrongly directed mind will do greater evil."
THE DHAMMAPADA

906 **Altruism** "The most sublime act is to set another before you."
WILLIAM BLAKE (1757–1827), ENGLAND

907 THE FOUR FRIENDS JATAKA

A story in a Buddhist *sutra* tells of four animal friends (illustrated). One day they decided to work out who was the eldest and thus the wisest. To determine their ages, they recalled their first memories of a nearby tree. The elephant remembered it as tall as himself, the monkey as a small tree, and the hare as a sapling. However, the bird remembered it as a seed, which he planted himself. In accordance with this, the animals set themselves in order, with the wisest highest, to show respect and harmony. The future Buddha was the bird, and the other animals were attendants and disciples.

---

908 A universal rule "That which we desire not for ourselves, do not do unto others."

JE GAMPOPA (1079–1153), TIBET

909 **A resolution** "We do good to ourselves by making and adhering to the resolution not to take advantage of others."
JE GAMPOPA (1079–1153), TIBET

910 **Forbearance** "If those people who are like wanton children are by nature prone to injure others, there's no use in being angry with them – that's like resenting fire for its heat."
SANTIDEVA (8TH CENTURY), INDIA

911 **Faith in hiding** "In spite of everything, I still believe that people are really good at heart."
ANNE FRANK (1929–1945), GERMANY

912 **Serve and protect** "Support living beings with your whole nature and protect them like your own body."
NAGARJUNA (c.150–250), INDIA

913 **No self, no other** "Do not err in this matter of self and other. Everything is Buddha, without exception."
FROM *THE WISDOM OF BUDDHISM*

914 **Understanding** "All things depend on something else. Thus, when enemies or friends are seen to act improperly, be serene and tell yourself, 'This is because of such and such.'"
SANTIDEVA (8TH CENTURY), INDIA

915 **Forgive easily** "'He reviled me, struck me, defeated me, robbed me.' In those who hold fast to such thoughts hatred will never cease."
THE DHAMMAPADA

916 **One family** "All men fear pain and death, all men love life. Remembering that he is one of them, let a man neither strike nor kill."
THE DHAMMAPADA

917 **Just desserts** "Whoever harms the harmless and offends the inoffensive, he will come to one of these misfortunes: he will have suffering, great loss, injury, severe illness, madness or trouble with authorities."
THE DHAMMAPADA

918 **Character index** "The best index of a person's character is how he treats people who can't do him any good and how he treats people who can't fight back."
ABIGAIL VAN BUREN (BORN 1918), USA

919 **Good friendships** "By attaching yourself to worthy people you yourself become worthy, as a creeper assumes the fragrance of the sandalwood tree."
LONGCHENPA (1308–1363), TIBET

920 **Doing harm** "He who injures or kills another and who longs for happiness will not find it for himself."
THE DHAMMAPADA

921 **Inadvertent** "He who wishes to secure the good of others, has already secured his own."
CONFUCIUS (551–479BCE), CHINA

922 **The inviolable law** "Reverence for human suffering and human life, for the smallest and most insignificant, must

be the inviolable law to rule the world. We must recognize that only a deep-seated change of heart, spreading from one man to another, can achieve such a thing in this world."
ALBERT SCHWEITZER (1875–1965), FRANCE/GABON

923   **Count to ten** "Let no man speak harshly to another. Angry speech brings trouble and blows in return."
THE DHAMMAPADA

924   **Hard lesson** "Everything that irritates us about others can lead us to an understanding of ourselves."
CARL JUNG (1875–1961), SWITZERLAND

925   **Rare strength** "If you master others, you are forceful. If you master yourself, you have inner strength."
LAO TZU (6TH CENTURY BCE), CHINA

RELATIONSHIPS

926   **Taking responsibility** "Your life is the fruit of your own doing. You have no one to blame but yourself."
JOSEPH CAMPBELL (1904–1987), USA

927   **Kindness to enemies** "In the cycle of existence that has neither beginning nor end, even my enemy has once been my father or mother and has added to my prosperity. Can I offer malice to repay kindness?"
LONGCHENPA (1308–1363), TIBET

928   **Understanding others** "I'm not angry with my bile and other humours, fertile source of pain and suffering! Why then resent my fellow creatures, victims too of such conditions?"
SANTIDEVA (8TH CENTURY), INDIA

929   **Inexpensive action** "Kind words do not cost much. Yet they accomplish much."
BLAISE PASCAL (1623–1662), FRANCE

930   A living thing "Society is a kind of organism whose component parts or units are most intimately related to one another in every conceivable way.

If any one part of it suffers damage in some form, the other parts are sure to share it sooner or later and in one way or another."

D.T. SUZUKI (1870–1966), JAPAN

931   Absolute necessities "Love and compassion are necessities, not luxuries. Without them, humanity cannot survive."

HIS HOLINESS THE 14TH DALAI LAMA (BORN 1934), TIBET

932   A painless truth "Nobody can hurt me without my permission."

MAHATMA GANDHI (1869–1948), INDIA

933   **A spiritual friend** "Whenever you see any sentient beings, look upon them as parents and children; avoiding all sinful company, put your trust in a spiritual friend."
ATISA (982–1054), TIBET

934   **The best response** "Answer with kindness when faced with hostility."
LAO TZU (6TH CENTURY BCE), CHINA

935   **Beyond family** "Neither father nor mother, nor relative, will do a man so much good as a well-directed mind."
THE DHAMMAPADA

936   **Seeing each other** "It is not our purpose to become each other; it is to recognize each other, to learn to see the other and respect him for what he is."
HERMANN HESSE (1877–1962), GERMANY

937 **The best in others** "Appreciation is a wonderful thing: it makes what is excellent in others belong to us as well."
VOLTAIRE (1694–1778), FRANCE

938 **True friendship** "The more we love our friends, the less we flatter them; it is by excusing nothing that pure love shows itself."
MOLIÈRE (1622–1767), FRANCE

939 **On higher ground** "Whenever anyone has offended me, I try to raise my soul so high that the offence cannot reach it."
RENÈ DESCARTES (1596–1650), FRANCE

940 **Communal rhythm** "We are like waves that do not move individually but rise and fall in rhythm. To share, to rise and fall in rhythm with life around us, is a spiritual necessity."
ALBERT SCHWEITZER (1875–1965), FRANCE/GABON

941 **SYMBOLS OF VICTORY**
In Buddhist legend, mysterious animals
appeared after the Buddha's awakening,
when all hatred vanished from the earth.
Animals that had been hunter and prey
mated with each other, and their hybrid
offspring, like those illustrated, symbolize
victory in the fight against disharmony.

---

942 **The three animals** The eight-legged lion has the body of a
lion, the head and wings of a garuda and claws at its knees
(his eight "legs" include these four claws). The fur-bearing
fish has the body of an otter with a fish's head and flippers.
The makara crocodile has a snail's shell, and its head is a
mixture of a dragon, a snake and a crocodile.

943 **Biblical harmony** "The wolf shall live with the lamb ... for
the earth shall be full of the knowledge of the Lord."
ISAIAH 11:6–9

SERVICE

944 **Respect your elders** "If a man has respect and courtesy for the aged, he will have long life, beauty, happiness and power."

THE DHAMMAPADA

945 **Immortality** "What we have done for ourselves alone dies with us; what we have done for others and the world remains and is immortal."

ALBERT PIKE (1809–1891), USA

946 **Wishing others well** "I would be a protector for those without protection, and a bridge for those desiring the farthest shore."

SANTIDEVA (8TH CENTURY), INDIA

947 **Virtue's fragrance** "Of little importance is the perfume of sandalwood, but the fragrance of virtue rises to heaven."

THE DHAMMAPADA

948 **Not in vain**
"If I can stop one heart from breaking,
I shall not live in vain.
If I can ease one life the aching,
Or cool one pain ..."
EMILY DICKINSON (1830–1886), USA

949 **Doing not dreaming** "The life of a
man consists not in seeing visions and in
dreaming dreams, but in active charity and
in willing service."
HENRY WADSWORTH LONGFELLOW (1807–1882), USA

950 **Some instructions** "Avoid defects, act correctly, work for a
goal; do not continue in purposeless actions, and always
cultivate your own talents."
ATISA (982–1054), TIBET

951 **Past merit** "By excellence of prior cause I have acted out of
virtue and merit in previous lives, and therefore I am not

now impoverished in food, clothing and the necessities. I am
naturally disposed to share my lot with others."

ATISA (982–1054), TIBET

952 **Directed mind** "The mind, imbued with love and compassion
in thought and deed, ought ever to be directed to the service
of all sentient beings."

JE GAMPOPA (1079–1153), TIBET

953 **Careful flight** "As the bee collects honey without destroying
the beauty and the scent of the flowers, so should the sage
go about the town."

THE DHAMMAPADA

954 **The call of compassion** "Bend thy
head and listen well, oh *bodhisattva* – compassion

speaks and says: 'Can there be bliss when all that lives must suffer? Shall you be saved and hear the whole world cry?'"

FROM *THE WISDOM OF BUDDHISM*

955 **Thinking of others** "The smallest amount of merit dedicated to the good of others is more precious than any amount of merit devoted to our own good."

JE GAMPOPA (1079–1153), TIBET

956 **Repeated blessing** "Blessed is he who speaks a kindness; thrice blessed is he who repeats it."

ARABIAN PROVERB

PEACE

957   **At ease** "Weak or strong, great or mighty, medium, short or small, seen and unseen, those living near and far away, those born and to be born – may all beings be at ease!"
THE METTA SUTTA

958   **Peace work** "If in our daily life we can smile, if we can be peaceful and happy, not only we but everyone will profit from it. This is the most basic kind of peace work."
THICH NHAT HANH (BORN 1926), VIETNAM/FRANCE

959   **Positive results** "A generous heart and wholesome actions lead to greater peace."
HIS HOLINESS THE 14TH DALAI LAMA (BORN 1934), TIBET

960   **Peace's clothing**
"For mercy has a human heart,
Pity, a human face:
And love, the human form divine,
And peace, the human dress."
WILLIAM BLAKE (1757–1827), ENGLAND

961 Heart's desire "Do you want long life and happiness? Seek peace, and pursue it with all your heart."
PSALMS 34:12,14

962 Presence, not absence "Peace is not an absence of war, it is a virtue, a state of mind, a disposition for benevolence, confidence, justice."
BARUCH SPINOZA (1632–1677), HOLLAND

963 Spreading peace "If there is harmony in the home, there will be order in the nation. If there is order in the nation, there will be peace in the world."
CHINESE PROVERB

964 Oneness "The peace which is the most important is that which comes to the souls of people when they realize their relationship, their oneness with the universe."
BLACK ELK (1863–1950), USA

965 **The general's surprise** "Do you know what astonished me most in the world? The inability of force to create anything. In the long run the sword is always beaten by the spirit."
NAPOLEON BUONAPARTE (1769–1821), FRANCE

966 **Human rights** "Peace, in the sense of the absence of war, is of little value to someone who is dying of hunger or cold. It will not remove the pain of torture. Peace can only last where human rights are respected, where people are fed and where individuals and nations are free."
HIS HOLINESS THE 14TH DALAI LAMA (BORN 1934), TIBET

967 **Peace and justice** "Peace is more important than all justice; and peace was not made for the sake of justice, but justice for the sake of peace."
MARTIN LUTHER (1483–1546), GERMANY

968 **Choose your enemies** "War with vices, but peace with individuals."
THOMAS HUGHES (1822–1896), ENGLAND

969 **Impossibility** "There was never a good war or a bad peace."
BENJAMIN FRANKLIN (1706–1790), USA

970 **Our best hope** "It is possible to live in peace."
MAHATMA GANDHI (1869–1948), INDIA

971 **One day** "We look forward to the time when the power of love will replace the love of power. Then will our world know the blessings of peace."
WILLIAM GLADSTONE (1809–1898), ENGLAND

972 **Good works** "All works of love are works of peace."
MOTHER TERESA (1910–1997), INDIA

973 **Beauty** "Peace is always beautiful."
WALT WHITMAN (1819–1892), USA

974 **Inner peace** "Without inner peace, it is impossible to have world peace."
HIS HOLINESS THE 14TH DALAI LAMA (BORN 1934), TIBET

GOVERNMENT

975 **A good soldier** "The best soldier fights without vengeance, without anger and without hate. He puts himself humbly below his comrades, thereby eliciting the highest loyalty from them. This is the power of non-belligerence and cooperation."

LAO TZU (6TH CENTURY BCE), CHINA

976 **Wrong freedom** "When the freedom they wished for most was the freedom from responsibility, then Athens ceased to be free and was never free again."

EDITH HAMILTON (1867–1963), USA

977 **Ideals for government** "I heartily accept the motto, 'That government is best which governs least,' and I should like to see it acted upon more rapidly and systematically. Carried out, it finally amounts to this, which I also believe, 'That government is best which governs not at all,' and when men are prepared for it, that will be the kind of government which they will have."

HENRY DAVID THOREAU (1817–1862), USA

978   **THE PILLAR EDICTS**
Asoka (or King Piyadasi) was an Indian king who ruled over much of south Asia. He is said to have renounced war and converted to Buddhism after witnessing the devastation caused during his conquest of nearby Kalinga. After his conversion he had a number of edicts inscribed on stone pillars, extolling the virtues of tolerance, peace and respect for all forms of life.

---

979   **Necessary virtue** "One who receives great gifts and yet is lacking in self-control, purity of heart, gratitude and firm devotion, such a person is mean."
ASOKA (c.304–232BCE), INDIA

980   **Tolerance** "All religions should live everywhere, for all of them desire self-control and purity of heart."
ASOKA (c.304–232BCE), INDIA

981 **Between faiths** "Whoever praises his own religion because of his excessive devotion, and condemns others with the thought, 'Let me glorify my own religion,' only harms his own religion. Contact between religions is good. One should listen to and respect the doctrines professed by others."
ASOKA (C.304–232BCE), INDIA

982 **Forgiveness** "Even those who do wrong should be forgiven where forgiveness is possible."
ASOKA (C.304–232BCE), INDIA

983 **Good and bad deeds** "People see only their good deeds saying, 'I have done this good deed.' But they do not see their evil deeds saying, 'I have done this evil deed.' or 'This is called evil.' We should think like this: 'It is these things that lead to evil, to violence, to cruelty, anger, pride and jealousy. Let me not ruin myself with these things.' And further, we should think: 'This leads to happiness in this world and the next.'"
ASOKA (C.304–232BCE), INDIA

984 **Good things** "Respect for mother and father is good; generosity to friends, acquaintances, relatives, brahmins and ascetics is good; not killing living beings is good."
ASOKA (c.304–232BCE), INDIA

985 **Wish list** "Dharma is good, but what constitutes Dharma? Little evil, much good, kindness, generosity, truthfulness and purity."
ASOKA (c.304–232BCE), INDIA

986 **Utopia** "When it shall be said in any country in the world, my people are happy; my jails are empty; the aged are not in want, the taxes are not oppressive … then may that country boast of its constitution and its government."
THOMAS PAINE (1737–1809), ENGLAND/USA

987 **Strong defences** "Concepts such as truth, justice and compassion cannot be dismissed as trite when these are often the only bulwarks which stand against ruthless power."
AUNG SAN SUU KYI (BORN 1945), MYANMAR

988 **Good governance** "To rule is easy, to govern difficult."
JOHANN WOLFGANG VON GOETHE (1749–1832), GERMANY

989 **Three ages** "It was once said that the moral test of a government is how that government treats those who are in the dawn of life, the children; those who are in the twilight of life, the elderly; and those who are in the shadows of life, the sick, the needy and the handicapped."
HUBERT H. HUMPHREY (1911–1978), USA

CHARITY

990 **Joy in good** "It is a good deed which needs no regrets and whose fruit is received with joy."
THE DHAMMAPADA

991 **The needs of all** "Wise people take the needs of all the people as their own. They are good to the good. But they are also good to those who are still absorbed in their own needs."
LAO TZU (6TH CENTURY BCE), CHINA

992 **Good deeds** "Charity is being a guide for the blind, cleansing those who hanker after desire, and purifying the suffering of anyone overcome or condemned by others."
ATISA (982–1054), TIBET

993 **A gift to God** "Charity never humiliated him who profited from

it, nor ever bound him by the chains of gratitude, as it was not to him but to God that the gift was made."
ANTOINE DE SAINT-EXUPÉRY (1900–1944), FRANCE

994 **No fear** "Where there is charity and wisdom, there is neither fear nor ignorance."
ST FRANCIS OF ASSISI (1181–1226), ITALY

995 **Closer and closer** "Prayer carries us half-way to God, fasting to the door of his palace. Giving alms procures us admission."
THE KORAN

996 **Real gains** "No act of kindness, however small, is ever wasted."
AESOP (620–560BCE), GREECE

997 **Harmless** "In charity there is no excess, neither can angel nor man come in danger by it."
FRANCIS BACON (1561–1626), ENGLAND

998   Building foundations "The more we expand our focus to include others' interests alongside our own, the more securely we build the foundations of our own happiness."
JE GAMPOPA (1079–1153), TIBET

999   Useless gifts "Though I have the gift of prophecy and understand all mysteries; though I have all faith, so that I could move mountains, and have not charity, I am nothing."
1 CORINTHIANS 13:2

1000   Advice from a Persian sage "Be humane and charitable; love your fellows; pardon those who have wronged you."
ZOROASTER (6TH CENTURY BCE), PERSIA

1001   Engine of wisdom "Just as a bird with unfledged wings cannot fly up into the sky, so without the power of wisdom, we cannot work for the good of others."
ATISA (982–1054), TIBET

GLOSSARY

Throughout the text the terminology used is Sanskrit (Sk) unless indicated as Pali (P) (used for the Pali canon or texts of the Theravada). Other terms appear in Japanese (J) or Tibetan (T).

anatta (P) Not-I. One of the three signs of being as defined by the Buddha, along with *anicca* (P, impermanence) and *dukkha* (P, suffering).

anicca (P) Impermanence. The reality that everything is in a continuous state of flux and change. Along with *anatta* (P) and *dukkha* (P) this is one of the three signs of being.

avidya Ignorance of the true nature of reality, which can be realized by transforming desire and anger and by letting go of self and selfishness. One of the Three Fires, it cannot be relinquished by an act of will, only through practice.

bhikkhu A Buddhist monk who has received higher ordination and is subject to the full discipline defined in the Vinaya Pitaka (the text which lays out the rules and framework of monastic life).

bhikshuni Buddhist nun.

bodhi Enlightenment, from the Sanskrit verb *budh*, to awaken.

bodhicitta Spirit of Awakening or Enlightenment Thought. Attainment of *bodhicitta* marks the shift in focus from self-concern to concern for the suffering for others manifesting itself as compassion (*karuna*) and a commitment to pursue the *bodhisattva* path.

bodhisattva Enlightenment being. In the Theravada this term refers to a single being striving to realize nirvana and become the next Buddha. In the Mahayana it defines the central ideal for all sentient beings, characterized by boundless compassion and a commitment to help all other beings realize Buddhahood.

Bon Ancient Tibetan religion which preceded Buddhism in Tibet, where it is still followed today.

brahma viharas literally, "the abodes of God", a sequence of four meditations recommended in the Brahmavihara Sutra: *metta* (loving kindness), *karuna* (compassion), *mudita* (altruistic joy) and *upeksha* (equanimity).

brahmin Historically, those born into the brahmin caste in India were held to be worthy of higher respect than other human beings. Buddhism used the term brahmin for everyone who attained enlightenment, to show that respect is earned not by birth, race or caste, but by spiritual effort.

Buddha An "awakened one", who is fully enlightened. One who attains nirvana without the benefit of another Buddha's teaching in his final lifetime.

Buddha, the Siddhartha Gautama (Gotama, P), the historical founder of Buddhism. The Buddha was born in present-day Nepal in the 5th century BCE. He lived and taught mostly in Northern India. His teachings, the Dharma, form the core of Buddhism.

Buddha-Dharma the religion of Buddhism.

dana Selfless giving. Commonly directed toward the Sangha, which brings merit, this is a central ideal of lay Buddhists.

Dharma (P, *Dhamma*) Buddhist teachings. This is a central Buddhist concept that includes the eternal truth that the Buddha realized, his verbal expression of that truth, and the phenomena or elements that comprise reality. Dharma is also defined in the Brahmanic/Hindu tradition as "duty", the moral order defining one's religious obligations in accordance with one's hereditary social status.

dhayana (P, *jhana*) "Meditative trance", a set of ascending levels of meditative absorption, numbering four or eight; also used to refer to meditation.

dukkha (P, *dukkha*) Suffering. The First Noble Truth states that all conditioned existence is characterized by suffering or unsatisfactoriness. With *anatta* and *anicca*, *dukkha* is one of the three signs of being.

guru A spiritual teacher who monitors a disciple's development and leads him or her toward final release from samsara. Translated as *lama* in Tibetan Buddhism.

Jakatas Teaching stories which each focus on one of the Buddha's previous lives. These texts are often quoted when monks instruct the laity.

kalpa Hindu and Buddhist eon, defined as approximately 4.32 billion years.

karma (P, *kamma*) An intentional action that has future consequences, including future rebirths. The consequences of past deeds largely determine one's general life situation.

karuna Compassion, an ideal associated with the Buddhas, central to the Mahayana *bodhisattva* path.

koan (J) Accounts of deeds or utterances of Zen masters, sometimes surprising in form and content. Used to further a student's enlightenment; central to

Rinzai Zen practice.

lama (T) Translation of guru (Sk). A master of meditation and ritual practice, who can teach and show others the way to enlightenment.

Mahasiddha "Great adept", a spiritually advanced figure associated with innovation in Tantric Buddhism.

Mahayana The Northern Tradition of Buddhism, so called because it spread north from its original location in Northern India.

mandala Cosmic symmetrical diagram, sometimes used in meditation to visualize spiritual realms and their inhabitants.

mantra Powerful words or sounds used in meditation, particularly in Tantric Buddhism.

mudras Symbolic hand gestures often used as aids to meditation.

nirvana (P, *nibbana*) The state of perfect enlightenment realized by Buddhas. Those who have gained this realization no longer accumulate karmic consequences and will no longer be reborn into samsara when they die.

paramitas The "perfections". *Bodhisattvas* are directed to cultivate a list of virtues or perfections. In the Theravada these are: generosity, morality, renunciation, wisdom, energy, patience, truthfulness, resolution, loving kindness, equanimity. The Mahayana tradition has six main *paramitas*, including meditation.

prajna (P, *panna*) Wisdom or insight, defined as the active capacity for spiritual discernment, "seeing into" the true nature of reality. This faculty is necessary for enlightenment and is central to all Buddhist schools.

samadhi Meditative practice leading to "one-pointed concentration" and bliss.

samsara The cycle of constant rebirth in which all beings are trapped as a result of their intentional deeds (*karma*). The cycle ranges from hell states to sublime, formless realms.

samyaksambodhi The "utterly complete" or "perfect" enlightenment realized by Buddhas.

Sangha The spiritual community of Buddhism.

satori (J) The experience of sudden awakening or enlightenment in Zen Buddhism.

siddha Accomplished spiritual adept with magical powers in Tantric Buddhism, often translated as "saint".

sila Moral practice (right speech, right action, right livelihood), the starting point of the Buddhist path.

skandhas The five components or aggregates that comprise a human being according to Buddhist analysis, including: physical body (*rupa*), feelings (*vendana*), perceptions (*samjna*), habitual mental dispositions (*samskaras*) and consciousness (*vijnana*).

stupa Buddhist holy building, a relic monument and a focus for devotion and merit-making.

sunyata Emptiness. Buddhist doctrine, found in nascent form in early Buddhism but central to Mahayana Buddhism, that asserts that even the dharmas, the conditioned elements of reality defined in the Abhidarma (higher doctrine), are devoid or empty of their own independent nature. Thus, seen from the perspective of absolute truth, the conventional distinction between nirvana and samsara is likewise void or empty. Also known as non-duality.

sutra (P, *sutta*) Discourse attributed to the Buddha and his early followers.

Theravada The Southern tradition of Buddhism.

Three Fires, the Desire, anger and delusion, negative energetic forces that can be transformed into positive attributes through Buddhist practice

Tripitaka (P, Tipitaka) The "three baskets" of the Buddha's authoritative teaching, including the monastic discipline (*vinaya*), discourses (*sutras*), and higher doctrine (Abhidarma). Also known as the Pali canon.

triratna The "three jewels" central to Buddhism: belief in the Buddha, the Dharma, and the Sangha.

Trishna (P, *tanha*) "Thirst" or "craving". The Second Noble Truth states that suffering (*dukkha*) arises because of craving or an attachment to sensual pleasures, to continued birth, and to non-existence.

Vajrayana The Tibetan tradition of Buddhism.

vihara Monastic residence.

vipashyana (P, *vipassana*) "Insight meditation", aims to discipline the mind while fostering a profound clarity about the nature of reality.

yoga Eastern spiritual discipline. One form of yoga aims at realizing the unity of the individual's soul and cosmic reality.

yogi Spiritual yogic master.

zazen (J) Seated Zen meditation.

FURTHER READING

Austin, John (ed.). *The Dhammapada*. London: Buddhist Society, 1945.

Ayya Khema. *Being Nobody, Going Nowhere*. Boston: Wisdom, 2002.

Bhikkhu Bodhi. *The Noble Eightfold Path*. Kandy: Buddhist Publication Society, 1998.

Cheetham, Eric. *The Great Way*. London: The Buddhist Society 1996.

Dalai Lama, H. H. the. *Essential Teachings*. London: Souvenir Press, 1995.

Harvey, Peter. *An Introduction to Buddhism*. Cambridge: Cambridge University Press, 1990.

Leggett, Trevor. *First Zen Reader*. North Clarendon, V.T.: Charles Tuttle, 1998.

Nyanatiloka Mahathera. *Buddhist Dictionary*. Kandy: Buddhist Publication Society, 1980.

Piyadassi Thera. *The Buddha's Ancient Path*. Kandy: Buddhist Publication Society, 1996.

Pema Chödrön. *Start Where You Are*. London: Element, 2005.

Tsongkhapa. *The Principal Teachings of Buddhism*. Howell, N.J.: Classics of Middle Asia, 1989.

Snelling, John. *The Buddhist Handbook*. London: Rider, 1998.

Suzuki, Shunryu. *Zen Mind, Beginner's Mind*. Boston: Weatherhill, 1973.

Ven. Myokyo-ni. *The Zen Way*. London: Zen Centre, 1977.

INDEX

ACKNOWLEDGMENTS

The publishers wish to thank the following for their kind permission to reproduce the copyright material in this book. Every effort has been made to trace copyright holders, but if anyone has been omitted we apologize and will, if informed, make corrections in any future edition. The publishers would also like to thank the following for help with translations from foreign texts: Jane Crediton, Dr Carl Maraspini, Dr Benedict Stolling, Rainer Wagner.

References are to "pearl numbers". **3** from *Hero with a Thousand Faces* by Joseph Campbell (Princeton University Press, 2004). Reprinted by permission of Princeton University Press; **5** from *The Creation of Consciousness: Jung's Myth for Modern Man* by Edward Edinger (Inner City Books, 1984). Reprinted by permission of Inner City Books; **48**, **149–151**, **204**, **212**, **257**, **278**, **417–423**, **430**, **433**, **462**, **470**, **545**, **567**, **571**, **573**, **700**, **760**, **785**, **812**, **835**, **838**, **843**, **847**, **851**, **857**, **885–8**, **919**, **927** from *Longchenpa: Kindly Bent to Ease Us – Part One: Mind*, translated and annotated by Herbert V. Guenther (Dharma Publishing 1975). Reprinted by permission of Dharma Publishing; **67**, **98**, **116**, **361**, **367**, **377**, **390**, **393**, **523**, **559**, **577**, **645**, **731**, **741**, **829**, **837** from *Glimpse after Glimpse* by Sogyal Rinpoche, published by Rider. Reprinted by permission of The Random House Group Ltd.; **69**, **74**, **90**, **92**, **95**, **114**, **156**, **236**, **238**, **241**, **309**, **313**, **319**, **330**, **351**, **354**, **541**, **544**, **547**, **579**, **722**, **788**, **866**, **868**, **877**, **904** from *The Buddha's Ancient Path* by Piyadassi Thera (Buddhist Publication Society, Kandy, Sri Lanka 1996). Reprinted by permission of the Buddhist Publication Society.; **71**, **145**, **146**, **157**, **178**, **200**, **250**, **255**, **264**, **306**, **342**, **343**, **405**, **480**, **489**, **515**, **519**, **522**, **531**, **561**, **588**, **607**, **625**, **910**, **914**, **928**, **946** excerpts from *A Guide to the Bodhisattva Way of Life* by Santideva, translated by Vesna A. Wallace and B. Alan Wallace. Copyright © 1997. Reprinted with the permission of Snow Lion Publications, www.snowlionpub.com; **75**, **102**, **175**, **191**, **245**, **260**, **272**, **294**, **325**, **328**, **406**, **429**, **434**, **458**, **475**, **581**, **600**, **672**, **729**, **742**, **876**, **899**, **931**, **955**, **966**, **974** reprinted by permission of The Office of His Holiness the Dalai Lama **100**, **184**, **201** reprinted by permission of Bryan Appleyard; **129**, **371**, **400**, **407**, **438**, **530**, **560**, **630**, **740** from *Advice from the Lotus Born: A collection of Padmasambhava's Advice to the Dakini Yeshe Tsogyal and other close disciples*, translated by Erik Pema Kunsang (Rangjung Yeshe Publications, Hong Kong 1994). Reprinted by permission of Rangjung Yeshe Publications; **162**, **388**, **410**, **456**, **628**, **642**, **771** reprinted by permission of The Trevor Leggett Group; **164**, **382**, **442**, **491**, **574**, **828** from *A Year with Thomas Merton: Daily Meditations from his Journals* (Harper 2004). Reprinted by permission of HarperCollins Publishers; **183**, **268**, **280**, **292**, **307**, **318**, **339**, **355**, **360**, **383**, **392**, **399**, **439**, **471**, **502**, **587**, **622**, **636**, **655**, **749**, **791**, **801**, **806**, **827**, **845**, **856**, **858**, **933**, **950**, **951**, **992**, **999** from *The Complete Works of Atisa*, translated by Richard Sherburne (Aditya Prakashan, New Delhi 2000). Reprinted by permission of the translator; **186** from *The Common Reader* by Virginia Woolf (1925). Reprinted by permission of the Society of Authors as the literary representative of the estate of Virginia Woolf. **214**, **707**, **830**, **901**, **909**, **952**, **955** from *Tibetan Yoga and Secret Doctrine* by Je Gampopa, translated by W.Y. Evans-Wentz (OUP, 2000). Reprinted by permission of Oxford University Press; **225**, **300**, **394**, **572**, **764**, **572**, **850**, **896**, **897** adapted from *Thus Have I Heard, Buddhist Parables and Stories*. Reprinted 1999 by The Corporate Body of the Buddha Educational Foundation, Taiwan. www.budaedu.org.tw; **320**, **372**, **376**, **440**, **464**, **466**, **635**, **737**, **759**, **775**, **792**, **821**, **880** from *Gems of Dharma, Jewels of Freedom* by Je Gampopa translated by Ken Holmes and Katia Holmes (Altea Publishing, 1995). Reprinted by permssion of the authors and Altea Publishing; **321**, **610**, **621**, **744**, **795**, **824**, **912** from *Master of Wisdom: Writings of the Buddhist Master Nagarjuna*, translations and studies by Christian Lindtner (Dharma Publishing 1986). Reprinted by permission of Dharma Publishing. **385** Copyright © 1999 by Wendell Berry from *A Timbered Choir*. Reprinted by permission of Shoemaker & Hoard Publishers; **398**, **505**, **954** from *Buddhist Texts through the Ages*, ed. Edward Conze (Bruno Cassirer 1954), reprinted in *The Wisdom of Buddhism* by Christmas Humphreys (Michael Joseph 1960); **412**, **656**, **862**, **930** reprinted by permission of The Buddhist Society, London; **427**, **507**, **637**, from *A Still Forest Pool: The Insight Meditation of Achaan Chah*, compiled by Jack Kornfield and Paul Breiter (Quest Books 1985). Reprinted by permission of Quest Books; **497** from *The Screwtape Letters* by C.S. Lewis copyright © C.S. Lewis Pte. Ltd. 1942. Extract reprinted by permission; **575**, **649**, **658**, **825**, **841** from *Tibetan Folk Tales* by Frederick and Audrey Hyde-Chambers © 1981. Reprinted by arrangement with Shambhala Publications, Inc., www.shambhala.com; **589**, **763** from *Autobiographies* by W.B. Yeats (Palgrave Macmillan, 1955). Reprinted by permission of A.P. Watt Ltd on behalf of Michael B. Yeats; **638** from *What the Buddha Taught* by Walpola Rahula (Atlantic Books 1986). Reprinted by permission of Grove Atlantic Press; **670**, **750** from *Buddhism in a Nutshell* by Narada Thera (Buddhist Publication Society, Kandy, Sri Lanka 1982). Reprinted by permission of the Buddhist Publication Society; **715** from *A Buddhist Spectrum: Contributions to Buddhist–Christian Dialogue* by Marco Pallis (World Wisdom, 2003). Reprinted by permission of World Wisdom, Inc.; **756** from *The Gospel for Asia*, trans. Kenneth Saunders (SPCK 1938), reprinted in *The Wisdom of Buddhism* by Christmas Humphreys (Michael Joseph 1960); **786**, **913** from *The Voice of the Silence*, trans. and annotated by "H.P.B." (Theosophical Publishing Co. 1889), reprinted in *The Wisdom of Buddhism* by Christmas Humphreys (Michael Joseph 1960); **892** Copyright © 1985 by Wendell Berry from *Collected Poems 1957-1982*. Reprinted by permission of Shoemaker & Hoard Publishers.

Picture credits: page 43 DBP archive.